Welcome

TO LET'S GO SEA FISHING – THE COMPLETE GUIDE!

It seems hard to believe, but time has rushed by so fast and we now have bookazine number three on the shelves. I have to say that Simon Everett and I have thoroughly enjoyed compiling it!

These publications encompass all that we're about – they show every reader what we truly love to do in simple and easy-to-understand terms.

This bookazine is the complete guide, because not only is it filled throughout with some superb fishing features, it is also a step-by-step guide on just how to go sea fishing. We've included all the knots you'll ever need to tie, the best rigs needed to improve your catch rate, the best baits to buy or collect and how to use them, a host of top tips and tricks and even sections on understanding how the weather affects our fishing!

We've also included the key target species that most of you like to catch, whether it's for sport, recreation or for the table – or all three.

A read through this will arm you with the information you need to approach your very next session at the right place, time and tide!

So chuck away the TV remote, pour yourself a cup of tea, then sit back and enjoy the read – let's go sea fishing together once again!

Tight lines,
Barney

Let's Go Sea FISHING
THE COMPLETE Guide

Copyright © 2013
Edited by Barney Wright & Simon Everett
Sub edited by Dean Kirkman
Designed by Bradley Sharp
Reprographics by Derek Mooney and Adam Mason

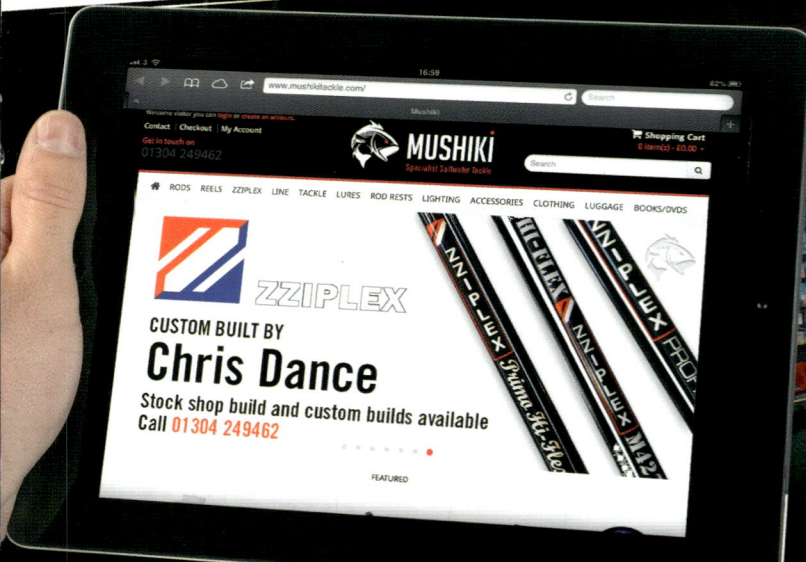

Contents

Night & Day

We challenge top northeast angler Gary Pye to catch from the same mark in daylight and darkness. Can he do it?

Meeting this challenge was definitely going to be interesting, and Gary would have to be on the ball to keep his confident promise of catching for the TSF camera.

The idea was to fish the same venue twice, once during daylight then again in the dark, in similar sea conditions, and compare the results. Gary chose to fish the Flat Rock, a well-known mark at Hawthorn, just to the north of Easington, in County Durham.

He just couldn't wait to get started so we met up with him at 8am and set off for Hawthorn. After a short drive and a steady half-hour walk along the coastal pathway from Seaham we arrived at the Flat Rock for 8.45am. The sea was relatively calm with only a little bit of a ground swell running in from the north and the wind had turned to a light westerly overnight.

SOD'S LAW

There was already another local angler on the Flat Rock when we arrived and he told us that he'd been fishing for about three hours without a single bite, let alone a fish. Gary wasn't put off, though,

and rigged up his Century TTR and Penn mag, loaded with 18lb Daiwa sensor and 80lb Sakuma shockleader. His first bait of the session, a rag and yellowtail lug cocktail on a 3/0 Sakuma Manta main hook with a 2/0 Manta Pennell hook, hit the water at around 9am.

Ten minutes passed and Gary's rod tip nodded – he picked it up and struck straight into a fish. The other guy looked on as Gary brought in a nice codling of just over 2lb, and even though he'd been there all that time without a bite, the guy was pleased to see a fish come in anyway.

SIZE MATTERS

After a couple of small bites on the next two casts, Gary decided to drop his main-hook size down to a 2/0 Gamakatsu G Point, to see if he could hook whatever was nicking his bait. So out went a nice fresh razorfish and black runnydown cocktail to tempt the little bait thieves.

It wasn't long before the bait was nabbed and so was the culprit. It was a small but beautifully coloured pouting, which, Gary pointed out, are appearing much more regularly along the northeast coast, as are dogfish and thornback rays.

TOP OF THE TIDE

With high tide fast approaching it was back to a 3/0 Pennell pulley rig loaded with yellowtail lug to try to tempt the codling. It wasn't long before one took the bait and, after getting snagged in the rocks and breaking free, Gary landed another codling around the 2lb mark.

With enough daylight left for one last cast, a black runnydown and ragworm bait was sent out in search of a better fish. The result, though, was another 2lb codling, bringing the bag for the daylight session to three codling and one pouting for 7lb 2oz.

During the day Gary took note of the features around the mark and any access points for getting down to the beach to land any bigger fish that his rod and reel might not be able to lift up the 15 to 20 feet drop from the Flat Rock itself. You should always check out points like this on any mark that's higher than beach level, for safety reasons as well as for retrieving fish. Also, if you intend to return in darkness, as we were, you will know exactly where you can and can't go.

IN THE DARK

We returned to the Flat Rock around 3pm the following week and prepared to fish through until nine or 10 o'clock. This time the sea conditions were about the same as they were on our day session but the wind was forecast to swing round to a light northerly.

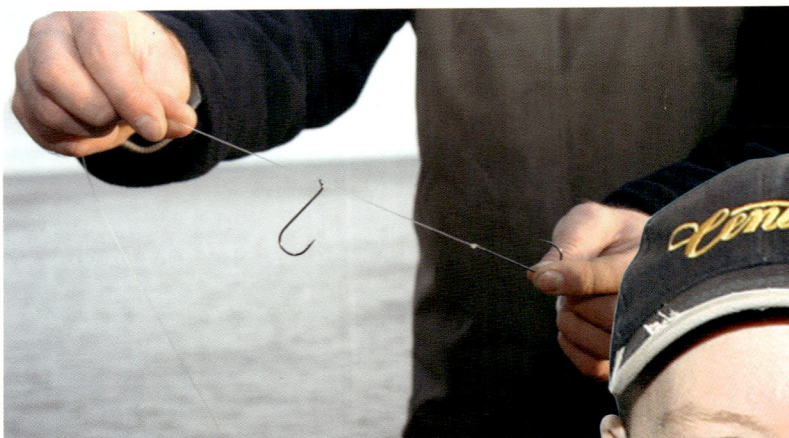

Big worm baits on a Pennel rig work best.

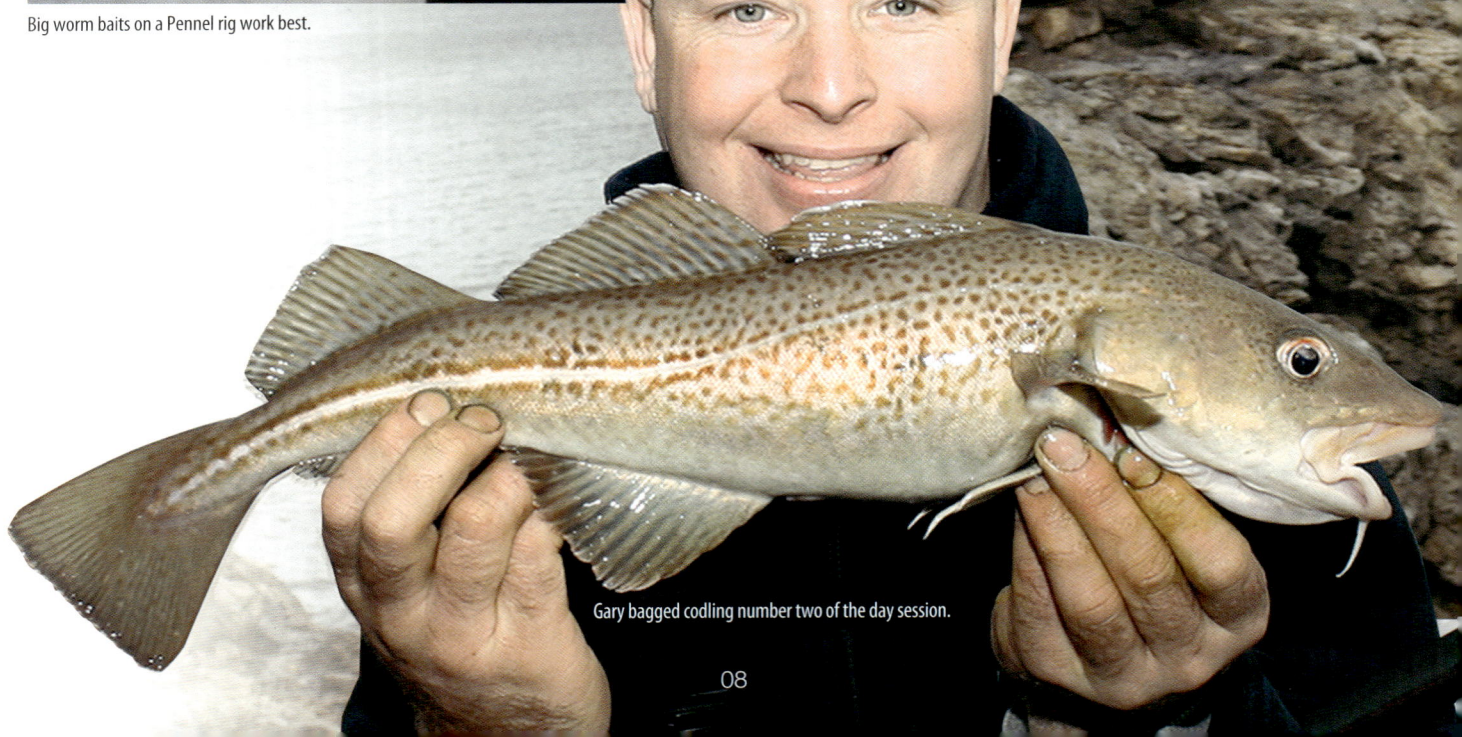

Gary bagged codling number two of the day session.

Gary swings in the first codling of the day session.

Changing to a smaller hook has resulted in this small pout.

A lug and razorfish cocktail.

By the time Gary had set his gear up it was just about dark, so using the same rod, reel and type of rig he sent a rag and lug cocktail bait out to the left of the rock. This was the area where some of the fish had come from during the daytime session.

A couple of casts later and well into darkness, Gary caught the first fish of the night, a small dab, which meant that his 'promise' would remain complete because he'd now caught on both sessions.

ROUGH TACTICS

After trying casts straight ahead and then to the right of the Flat Rock without success, Gary decided that the really rough ground to the left must be where the cod would be. With that in mind and high water looming he put the next rag and lug bait right into the rough stuff.

Almost immediately the rod signalled the typical nod of a cod bite. Gary picked up the rod and a few seconds later he was into a nice fish, a codling of 3lb 8oz. "It looks like the right spot so I'll keep the bait over there," he said, and put the next cast in the same direction. "Fishing among these rocks is not for the faint-hearted, though, because it's exceptionally rough

A plump dab adds another species to the tally.

ground, with maybe six or seven out of 10 leads lost – not my idea of fun!"

THEY'RE GETTING BIGGER

Another good bite hit the TTR. Gary struck and said: "This is a better fish," then his worst nightmare occurred – he became stuck solid in the rocks. After unsuccessfully trying slack line a few times he managed to snap the rotten bottom, losing his 7oz lead but freeing the fish. This one had to be pulled up by hand and weighed a very respectable 5lb 8oz.

So a small dab and two good codling had taken the night session nearly 2lb 8oz ahead of the day session… for the present!

OH MY… COD!

High water was now upon us and, as Gary well knows, this particular mark fishes pretty well over the top of the tide and an hour or two back. Sticking to the left again, Gary cast out a nice lug and rag bait and rested the rod on the tripod while he baited up his spare rig.

All of a sudden Gary dropped the trace and ran for his rod, which had just about been pulled out of the stand. As he took up the slack line, the rod tip lunged over as the fish made a run for it.

Gary shouted: "This is a double-figure cod!" For the first minute or two he could only hold the rod as the fish took line off his Penn 525, then he began to get control of the fish and gain some ground on it. We could see that this was definitely a big fish because a Century TTR doesn't bend easily and this one was bent over nicely. We were watching

and thinking: "Please don't get stuck in those rocks," and we could see that Gary was thinking exactly the same, but none of us dared say it out loud.

Gary took his time and after a good 10 minutes he struggled to wind the reel as the fish got into the undertow at the front of the Flat Rock, then in the wide beam of his Tiga lamp we caught the first glimpse of a huge cod. After carefully landing the fish on the rocks beneath us he then handed over the rod while he climbed down to the beach to retrieve the fish.

A few minutes later Gary passed the massive cod up to us and made his way back up onto the rock. He could hardly believe his eyes when he took a proper look at the fish and was absolutely delighted with his catch.

The fish weighed in at 14lb 7oz 12dr, a very well-deserved personal best for a very skilful and dedicated angler. The final bag weight for the night was around 24lb, beating the daylight session by more than 16lb.

Top tips

If you're receiving bites but not hooking fish, try dropping down your hook sizes.

Stop being spiked by the grip leads in your tackle bag by carrying the grip wires and a pair of pliers. It only takes a minute or two to wire your leads as you use them.

Vary your bait combinations until you find what works best at the mark you're fishing.

For night fishing, make sure you have a fully charged reliable lamp and a small led lightweight lamp as a spare.

If you have a spare rod it's a good idea to take it with you, especially if you're fishing a match. A dropped rod could mean a breakage to the rod guides or even the blank and then you can't continue fishing.

The smile says it all. These smashing cod prove that Gary's done it again for the Let's Go camera.

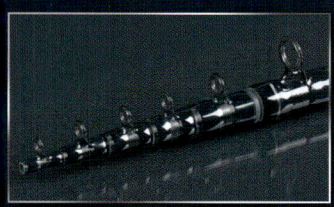

The Pulley Rig

We reveal some of the best sea angling traces for you to use.

The pulley rig seems to have originated in both South Wales and the northeast of England around 20 years ago.

The initial pulley principle idea was taken from the standard sliding-leger rig but changed to fish as a normal fixed paternoster rig would. The pulley idea was thought up as anglers in the two named areas were fishing rough ground on a day-to-day basis. They were losing gear and fish when using traditional paternoster rigs due to the trailing lead snagging in the rough ground as the rig or fish was being retrieved.

Although initially designed for rough ground, it also became popular with anglers fishing the shore for rays and tope over clean ground, albeit in a much-modified form.

How It Works

The main advantage of the pulley rig is that when a fish takes the bait, it has the power to pull the hooklength and rig body through the pulley-rig bead and physically lift the lead up out of the snags.

Once the rig body is pulled through the swivel, until it hits the bead above the Impact Shield, the lead is up in the water and above the snags.

The pulley rig works best when casting into a good depth of water. When fishing at range in shallow water the rig lays too flat on the sea bed, and as a fish takes the bait and pulls against the lead, this action can drag a lead deep into a snag.

In deep water, due to the raised angle of the line, the lead tends to literally lift upwards and out of a snag. Pulley rigs are not a good choice for very shallow-water fishing!

Due to the pulley principle the rig also acts as a self-striking rig. As the fish takes the bait it can pull only minimum line before it comes up tight against the full weight of the rising and sliding lead. It's the weight of the lead that creates the self-striking effect.

Another attribute of the pulley rig is that it can be made to a longer length than other rigs, but remains only half its total length for casting. This means that when the lead reaches the stop bead you have a full length of heavy mono that resists abrasion from fish with rough skin, rocks and barnacles when retrieving big fish over rough ground. ▶

Build Sequence

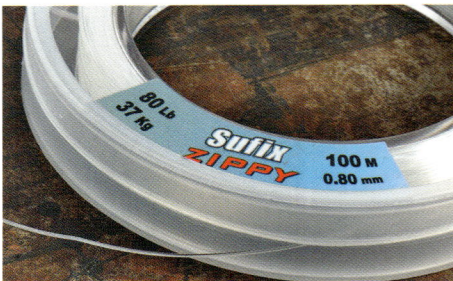
Start with 50 inches of 80lb rig-body line.

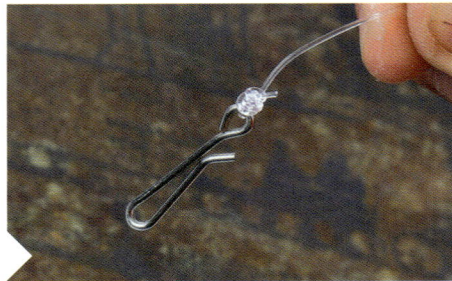
To one end of the rig body, tie on a Gemini lead link.

Slide on a Breakaway Impact Shield followed by a 3mm bead and crimp. Leave around one-and-a-half millimetres for the Impact Shield to slide, to avoid hook-snood stretch during the cast.

Above the crimp, slide on a 5mm bead, a Fox pulley-rig bead and another 5mm bead.

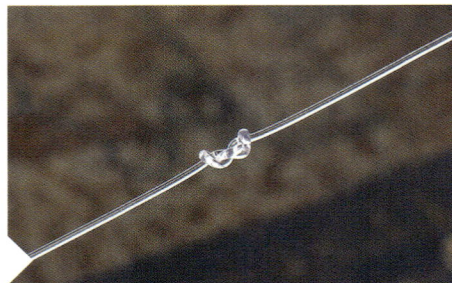
Measure the free end of line, leaving it slightly shorter than the main rig body, and tie a double figure-of-eight knot in it to form the hooklength.

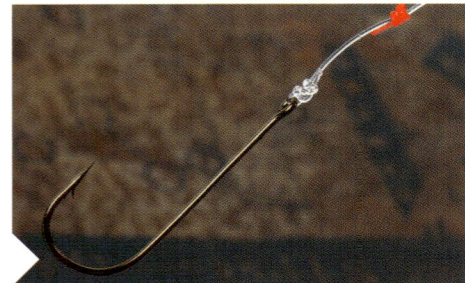
Tie on either a single size 4/0 Viking pattern hook for rays or, alternatively, us a 3/0 or 4/0 two-hook Pennel rig. When using a single hook, tie in, above the hook, a Powergum sliding stop knot to act as a bait stop when casting.

Most anglers choose to build this rig incorrectly by replacing the more expensive pulley-rig bead with a standard-eyed swivel, but powerful casters have found that when using a standard swivel the thin diameter wire of the eye concentrates pressure on the same tiny section of rig body with every cast. This weakens this section of the line and, inevitably, it will part. This occurs during the main power of the cast, resulting in rig-body breakage and the lead weight flying down the beach and causing a potential injury, or fatality, to anybody in the firing line.

The rig described with the Impact Shield is designed when maximum-range casting is required. To save on rig components when tackle losses will be heavy and distance is less important, do away with the Impact Shield assembly altogether and replace the Gemini lead link with a Gemini bait clip. The hook then just sits in the bait clip, but this rig will not fly as far due to the increased air friction of the bait and not being streamlined by the shield.

When fishing mixed rough ground with heavier 30lb reel line and using a weak-link system to the lead weight, you can also reduce losses by putting a swivel where the figure-of-eight knot should go on the rig body, then adding a hook snood slightly lighter than your main reel line. This will break should the hook get snagged, but remember that a lighter hook snood may also cost you fish.

Want More?
Check out *www.totalseamagazine.com* for rig-making videos and more.

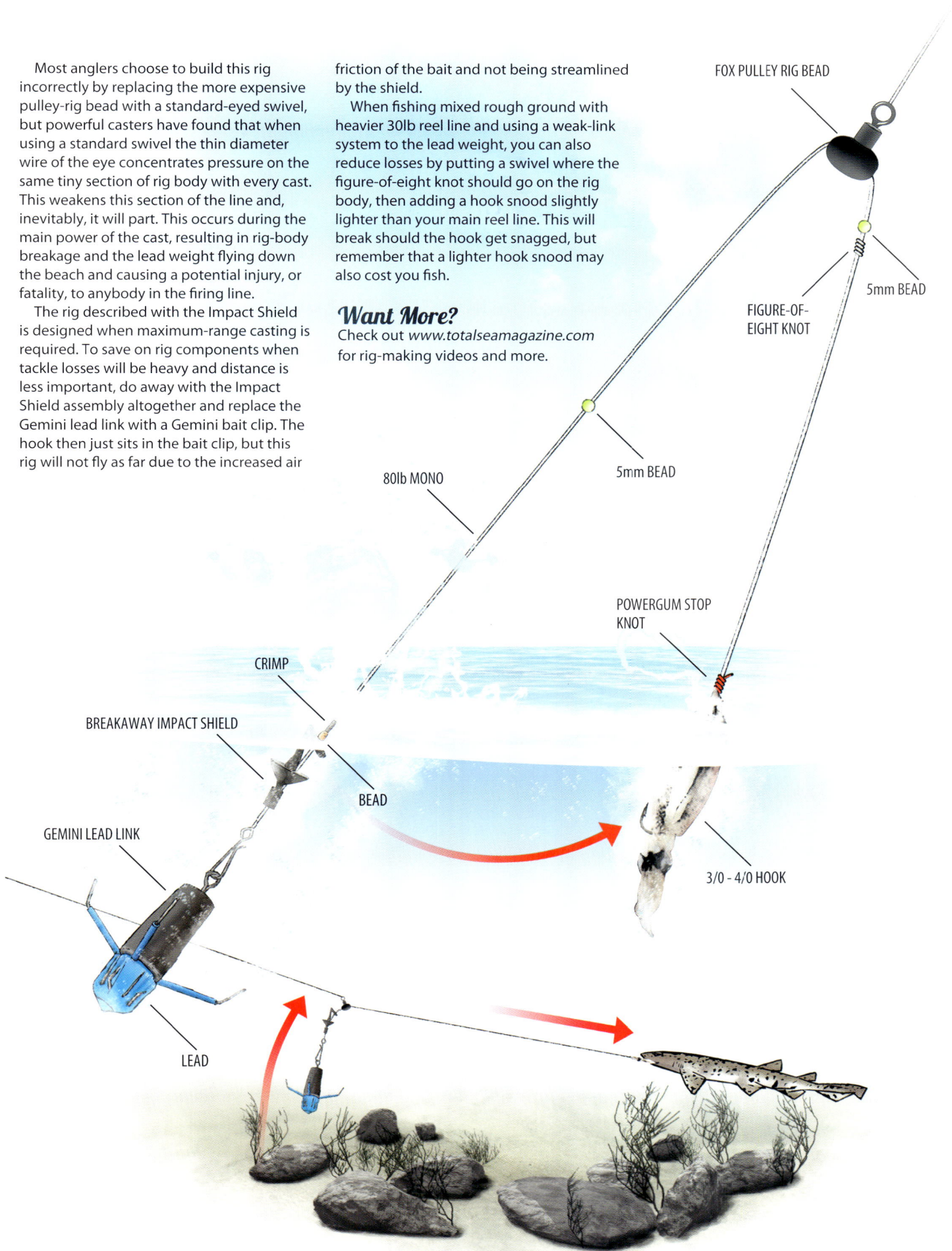

FOX PULLEY RIG BEAD

5mm BEAD

FIGURE-OF-EIGHT KNOT

80lb MONO

5mm BEAD

POWERGUM STOP KNOT

CRIMP

BREAKAWAY IMPACT SHIELD

BEAD

GEMINI LEAD LINK

3/0 - 4/0 HOOK

LEAD

13

The Half-Blood

Learn how to tie the reliable half-blood knot with this essential step-by-step guide.

With a multitude of knots used for angling, choosing which one to use and then knowing how to tie it can be a nightmare.

Simple, multi-purpose knots make life so much easier and one example is the tried-and-tested half-blood knot, which has several uses including attaching the line to a hook, swivel or link.

The half-blood is probably the first fishing knot most of us learn to tie. It is best used with monofilament lines as braid tends to be slippery and needs more complicated multi-turn knots.

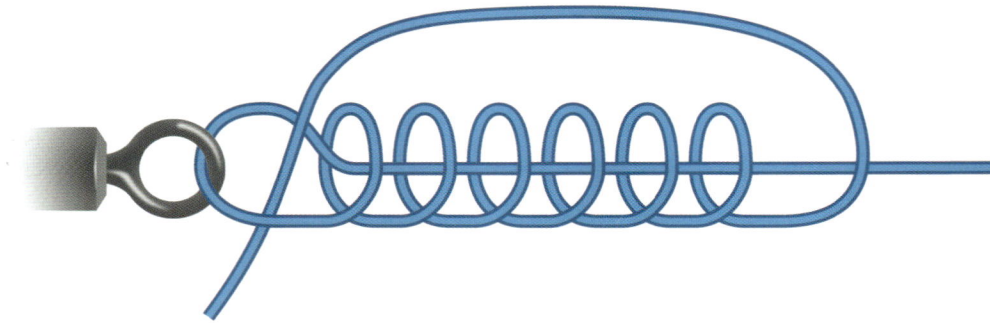

Top tips

The half-blood is excellent for tying hook night as it's so easy to do that, with practice can be done with your eyes closed.

Leave a 1cm tag to allow for any slippage.

Thin lines, such as 10lb strain, need six to eight turns in the loop but three or four turns is ample for 50lb lines.

For extra strength you can pass the line through the hook eye twice before making the knot.

How To Tie A Half-Blood Knot

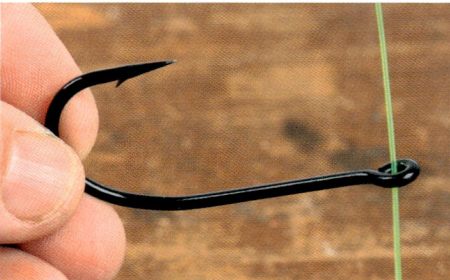

Pass the tag end through the hook eye.

Make four to eight twists, depending on line diameter.

Pass the tag end through the loop formed above the hook eye.

Lubricate the line with saliva.

Pull the running line smoothly and the coils will bunch up tight.

Trim so that there's one centimetre of tag left and it's job done!

Understanding Tides

TSF explains how Mother Nature affects our fishing…

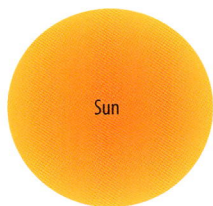

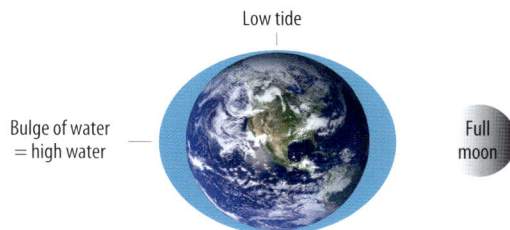

Low tide

Bulge of water = high water

Sun

Full moon

Low tide

Sun

New moon

Bulge of water = high water

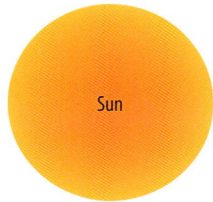

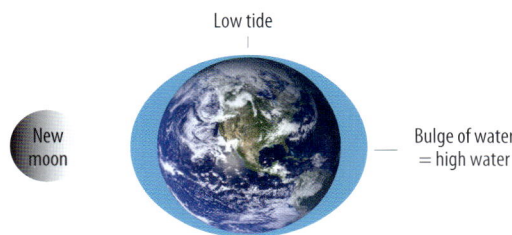

Tides are vitally important to anglers. They govern the movement and whereabouts of fish, dictate when and how we collect bait, tell us when we can and cannot launch our boats and in many areas govern the actual marks we are able to fish. It sounds complicated, but a basic understanding of how the tides work is relatively easy.

Tides are caused by the effects of gravity within the configuration of the earth, the moon and the sun, as well as the planet's movements. A good way to understand this is to imagine that the earth is completely covered in water.

There are two outward bulges of water, one pulled towards the moon on one side of the earth, with the other on the opposite side of the planet created by the earth's centrifugal rotation. The rise and fall in sea levels are caused by the earth rotating on its axis underneath these bulges of water. There are two tides every day because the earth passes under the two bulges as it rotates within its 24-hour cycle. These are called lunar tides.

Two additional bulges of water are also caused by the sun, and are called solar tides. These work with the lunar tide during the new and full-moon period as the earth, moon and sun are in line and both bulges of water then coincide in the same place on the earth's surface, creating the larger spring tides.

When the earth, moon and sun are at a right angle to each other and the direct pull is much reduced, the high water caused by the lunar tide coincides with the low water of the solar tide, and gives us the smaller neap tides.

You might wonder why the time of high water is not the same all around the UK. The difference in tide times is due to the land mass getting in the way of the moving tidal current. As the earth rotates, water moves over the earth's surface to create the high tides, but due to the shape of the coastline and the differences in overall sea depth, there is a time delay. With all areas of coastline having different physical terrain and massively varied depths, it's this that gives each area its own specific tidal pattern.

The highest tides of the year fall a day or two after the full and new moon nearest to the spring equinox, usually around March 20th/21st, and the autumn equinox on September 22nd/23rd. The equinox is when the tilt of the earth's axis is angled neither away from, nor towards the sun, the centre of the sun being in the same plane as the earth's equator. Some years have higher tides than is usual, and 2015 is a year we'll see these unusually big tides.

Tides occur roughly every 12 hours and 25 minutes in the UK. It's not exactly 12 hours, or half the time of an earth day, as you would expect. This is due to the moon also orbiting around the earth and exerting its effect on the bulge of water, requiring the earth to rotate for an extra 25 minutes to compensate, to be directly under the high-water bulge.

That is all there is to tides. Once you understand the earth's rotation and the bulges of water, the rest is easy!

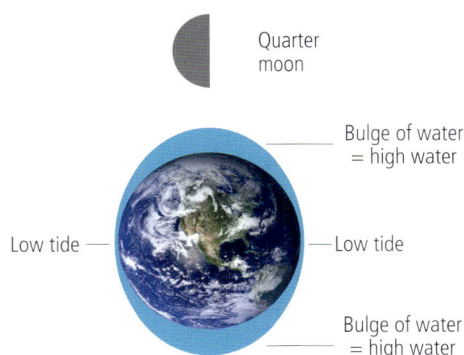

Quarter moon

Bulge of water = high water

Sun

Low tide

Low tide

Bulge of water = high water

A cracking 7lb bass for Barney Wright!

My Bonus Bass

Barney Wright ventures to his favourite beach to film a casting tutorial and ends up catching a bass on almost every cast.

Red-letter days often happen when you least expect them. I've lost count of the times I've travelled to venues, the adrenaline pumping from the vivid images of the fantastic sport on offer, only to be told the worst six words in angling: "You should have been here yesterday." And then there are other trips with no real agenda or expectations that are suddenly transformed into epic sessions.

That's why a recent visit to my beloved stretch of beach – the coastline at Eccles on Sea, in Norfolk – will stick in my mind for a long while. It was one of the most uncanny outings I can remember, because I landed four bass in five casts and all achieved with little concentration.

THE VENUE

The journey took me via Lowestoft to pick up some peeler crabs and squid from Pakefield tackle shop Angling Mad.

The information coming in was that the fish were being caught at Cart Gap, which sits on the north side of Eccles and has a large slipway where boats are launched – and sometimes jet skis, which cause no end of bother for anglers. I had been told shoals of bass had started to roam the area looking for peeler crabs – a prey that can really send them into a feeding frenzy.

As I pulled into the pay-and-display car park, I noticed plenty of anglers off-loading their gear – the word was well and truly out that the bass were in. So I wandered down the slipway to have a look at the conditions and how busy the beach was – I haven't seen so many anglers set up here in years! I usually have the beach to myself, but this time it was a matter of finding a spot. Usually I would fish south of this mark, somewhere halfway along the Eccles stretch. The beach faces roughly northeast and, since there was a howling northeasterly wind, the sea was

A crab-and-squid bait is pushed more than 100 yards into a strong headwind.

reaching the defence, making it hard to set up anywhere else but here or down at the Sea Palling reefs at the south end of Eccles.

NOT MUCH SPACE

The beach was pretty much full to the north, but no-one had set up immediately south of the slipway – probably because they were worried about being washed off the beach! But I knew we were only on very small tides and able to fish in safety.

It was about four hours into the flood, which left two more for me to fish, plus a couple of hours down. This is the perfect time to fish here and was why so many anglers had turned up in unison.

TACKLE AND TACTICS

There's a sand bar that sits about 100 yards out and consequently a big gulley that runs from it, right to the shore. I know that the bass feed along the sand bar, and since the sea was rough, food particles would be dislodged. There was also an early glut of peeler crabs, which the bass were feasting on.

I decided that I would try to fish the sand bar to start off with and, as there was a 25mph wind in my face, I used two rods that were capable of blasting a bait to range in the conditions. To assist the long-distance casting I used two Daiwa 7HT Turbo reels that

How To Peel A Crab

Look for crabs that are showing the signs of cracks along their edge because these are ready to peel.

Start by removing the legs.

Peel away the undercarriage.

Be sure to remove as much shell as possible because just a small piece could mask the hook.

Once the underside is cleared, pull away the main shell.

Finally, remove the mouth pieces.

The finished job – a crab devoid of shell and ready for baiting up.

This small bass is cross, showing off its array of weaponry!

were loaded with Ultima Power Steel 12lb line and attached to an 80lb shockleader.

My rigs were straightforward – both consisted of a size 3/0 Pennel hook setup. One was a simple paternoster with a 30in fluorocarbon snood, and the other was an up-and-over trace with a 48in snood.

BAITING UP

My plan was to fish with a peeler-crab-and-squid cocktail – although using a whole squid, or even straight crab, was tempting. I felt confident that a cocktail would give a greater scent trail and the bass a little variety. My baiting method was simple – peel a crab, cut it in half, thread it up the hook and whip

on a strip of squid alongside it.

A LONG FIRST CAST… TIME-WISE!

First up was the paternoster rig that, because the bait was streamlined and also clipped down to punch the wind, I pushed out to the sand bar quite easily.

With that task completed it was a case of getting down to the main job in hand – putting together a step-by-step sequence of my ground cast for the next issue of the magazine. This took about an hour or so and I hadn't really been watching my other rod for bites – though I did look every now and then to make sure a lunker hadn't whipped it off the rest!

During this time an angler along the beach, Simon Farrow from Dereham, in Norfolk, had bagged on plain lugworm a codling that was just 60 yards out!

I noticed that the line on my rod was going a little slack and then tightening again, but since there was weed present I thought nothing of it. The surprise was that, when I reeled in, what I thought was weed was in fact a bass of about 1½lb – what a great start!

UP TO SPEED

Now that I had both rods in use, I was all out to bag a better fish and really wanted one over 5lb.

The long up-and-over trace was baited the same way as the paternoster, and then out to the sand bar it went – closely followed by the rebaited rig, which I pushed out just a little further and just beyond the bar. I wanted to try to keep away from the schoolies and cover as much ground as possible to seek out the better fish.

With two rods out, I sat back on the box, rubbed my hands together and beamed out a smile; I had a really good feeling about the day.

HARD TO SEE

Identifying bites was fun because the weed in the waves was continually pulling down on the line, then, once free from the wave, would send it pinging back up. To the untrained eye, this could look like a bite, but the difference with a real bite is any irregularity in the rod-tip movement, as it will bounce out of sequence with the wave pattern. Because I was fishing at range, I had to watch the tips closely to spot any movement in them signifying a fish.

About 20 minutes passed and I saw a slight knock – then a pull

How To Bait Up A Pennel Rig With Crab And Squid

Using scissors, cut the crab in half like this, but not all the way through.

Weave the hook through the body.

Tip hook a slice of squid.

Run the squid alongside the crab and hook.

Bind the cocktail using bait elastic – but not too tight.

Wrap the snood line three or four times around the top hook.

Pass the top hook through the top of the bait and that's job done!

The beach at Eccles had plenty of rods present that day!

A very happy Barney removes the hooks from his fish.

over and slack line. This was a classic bass bite and I reeled in hard as the fish swam towards me – they tend to do this.

A BETTER FISH

As the fish neared the surf it began to pull a little, albeit not very hard. This was not the fish I wanted, but it was certainly a result to have had two fish in two casts! This bass was about 2lb, a little bigger than the first, and it had taken the long trace on the inside of the sand bar. Another 20 minutes passed and the rod that I cast over the bar showed

nothing at all, whereas the rod on the inside was getting regular tugs. So I felt it prudent to bring in the long rod and cast fresh bait on the inside of the sand bar, as it appeared that the fish were feeding on the shore side of it and also in the gulley.

WHACK!

I had both baits inside the sand bar and was just sitting down to film another section for the website, when I heard a crash and looked up to see my rod rocking like a seesaw in the rest. Something had hit my bait hard, crashed the reel against the tripod leg and driven the rod's butt ring into the rest's cup! Thank goodness for the rod ring, because without it my rod would

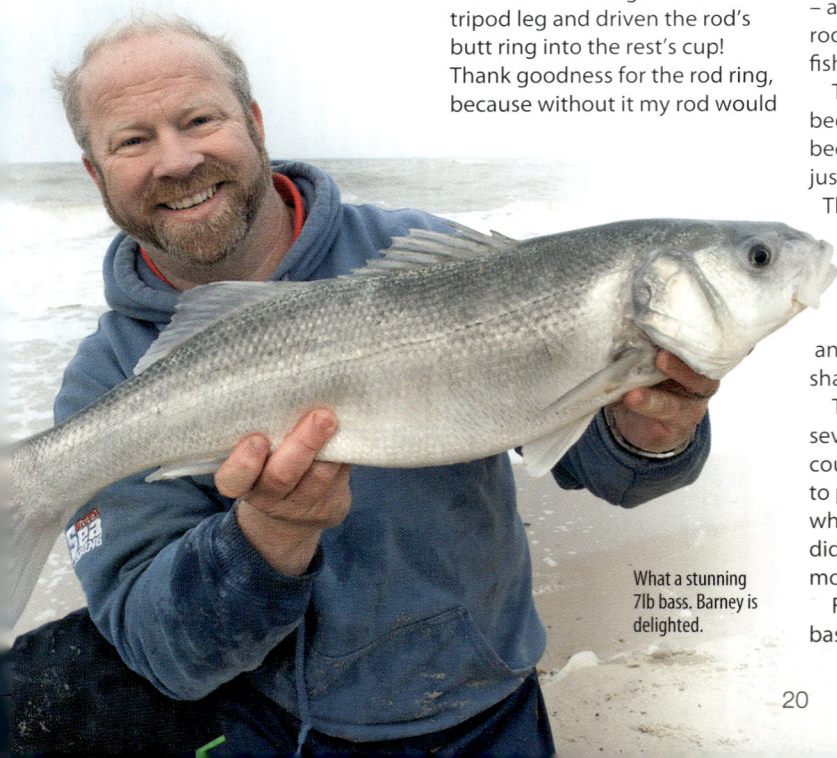

What a stunning 7lb bass. Barney is delighted.

have been lost. I hadn't loosened my drag – a big mistake – but thankfully I got away with it. I ran over and grabbed the rod – the line was loose and I had to reel in frantically to catch up with the fish.

It wasn't until a drop-off at the beginning of the surf tables that I finally caught up with the bass – and a few heavy thuds on the rod soon revealed it was the big fish I had hoped for.

The nerves started to set in because, although the take had been savage, you always wonder just how good the hook-hold is.

The bass was certainly using the tide and surf to its advantage – every time I got it near to the sandy ledge, it pulled really hard and refused to come into the shallows.

The battle continued for several minutes, and although I could have bullied it, I decided to play it safe and gave line when the fish wanted it. I just didn't want any heart-breaking moments.

Finally I managed to get the bass over the gutter and that

was when I first saw it. I still had to be patient and wait for a suitable wave to bring the fish towards me. And then there it was in all its glory – a stunningly beautiful bass, which pulled the scales almost to the 7lb mark. What a way to end a perfect session.

IT'S NOT OVER YET

Throughout all the excitement I completely ignored my other rod, which was quietly bouncing away – I had another fish on, a fourth bass of about 2½lb. It must have been on the line for a little while as it had a clear attack mark on its tail end from a bigger fish. Nevertheless it went back and swam away quite happily.

Although I could have carried on, I had other fish to fry – so to speak – so decided to call it a day. I was only going to keep the one fish anyway. It would have been nice to have returned to the beach 24 hours later and have someone say: "You should have been here yesterday." At least I would have been able to give that rarest of replies… "I was!"

BASS & SURF

ZEBCO EUROPE

QUANTUM® Sea

WORLD CHAMPION SURF
The perfect fighting machine for the surf angler who is only satisfied with the best of the best. The long cast spool enables maximum casting distances.

ALPS™

BASS BASHA
Top spinning rod for use on the shore or beyond, with extremely quick and stiff action. Ideally suited for launching wobblers, rubber baits and spoons long distances into the wind.

WORLD CHAMPION SURF III
The acceleration is sensational while the powerful backbone won over the test anglers immediately. The ring configuration enables "world class" casting distances with both monofilament and the increasingly popular braided lines.

All rods

EPOXY COATED

SIC GUIDES

CSC

Hot Sauce

Saltgard

14

CONTINUOUS ANTI-REVERSE

10

CONTINUOUS ANTI-REVERSE

PT MAGNUM

SMOKE INSHORE
Perfect mid-sized spinning reels for sea anglers – whether for bass, cod or sea trout. The special production methods and materials ensure extreme corrosion resistance even with frequent use in the marine environment.

Understanding Isobars

David Hall explains how Mother Nature affects our fishing…

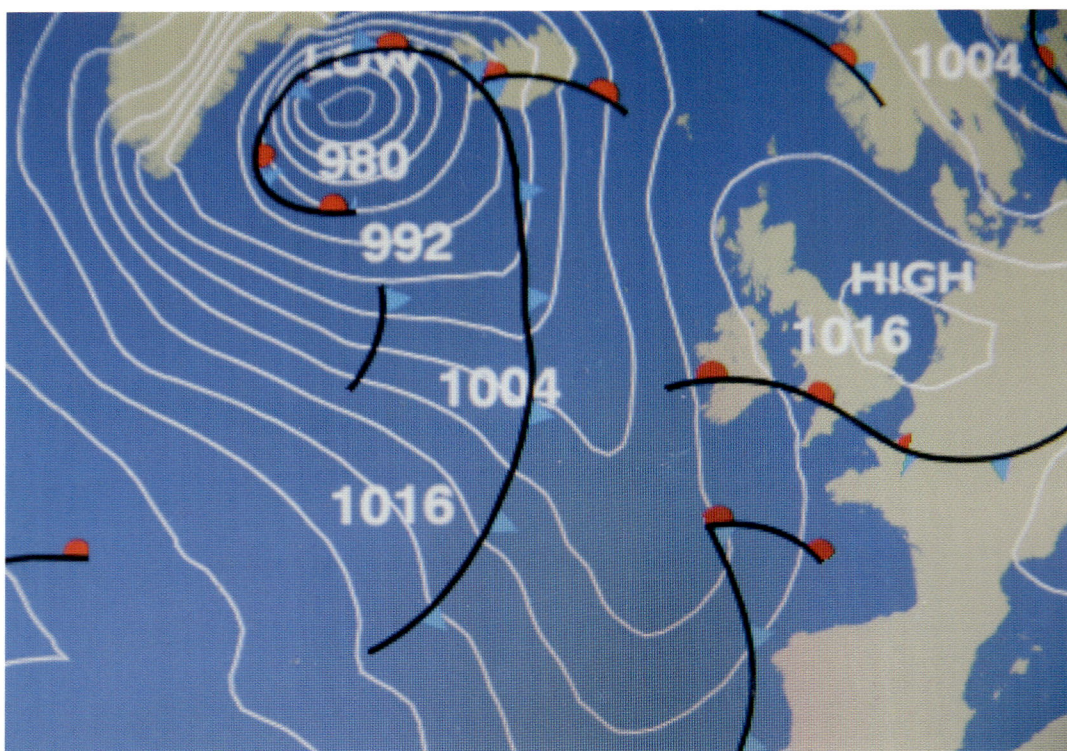

WIDE LINES – LOW WIND; TIGHT LINES – HIGH WIND

It's the spacings between the isobars that forecast just how severe the wind is likely to be. If the isobars are wide apart, then wind strengths will be light, generally, and good weather can be anticipated. If the isobars are packed in tight very closely together, then the wind strength will be strong or gale force and this is a weather depression moving in that's likely to bring heavy rain too.

The isobar lines can often be packed tightest around the centre of the depression, indicating where the strongest winds will be. We can visually see this if we watch a prolonged, in-depth forecast on the TV, or view the forecast isobar pressure patterns on the internet. By doing this alongside basic geography, we can see if the marks we want to fish fall in the higher or lower wind areas within that time span as a depression moves across Ireland and the UK.

WIND CIRCLES

An interesting thing to know is that, in the northern hemisphere, including the UK, winds blow anti-clockwise around an advancing low-pressure weather system, but clockwise around a high-pressure system. The wind will also flow in an almost parallel line with the isobars, which gives us the ability to forecast wind direction as the system moves over the country.

Learning a little about isobars then tells us a lot about what the weather is doing and where, when and even if we should fish at all!

Those of you using the TV or internet for a weather forecast prior to fishing will sometimes see a diagram of the North Atlantic, or sometimes just the UK and Ireland, with circular lines drawn on it. These lines are isobars and they foretell the direction and severity of the wind.

An isobar is a line joining areas of equal atmospheric pressure. If you look at each line it will have a number either on, over or under it. This number will decrease or increase by four with each isobar. This number measures the atmospheric pressure in millibars (mb), which equates to 0.02953 inches of mercury.

An exceptionally low pressure forecasting hurricane conditions would read as low as 860mb as an example, whereas an anti-cyclone high-pressure system bringing good, settled weather could see a reading as high as 1,060mb.

Typical UK readings would be 980mb to 1,020mb, but the average sea-level pressure is 1,013mb. The centre of deep depression could read as low as 950mb, but 930mb has been recorded in the UK in the past. These isobar line readings are adjusted to sea level with any differences due to altitude being ignored.

Look at an area of high pressure, and the millibar number will be highest in the centre of the innermost circle with numbers on the circular lines outside getting lower. When a low-pressure system approaches, the innermost circle will have a lower reading with the outer-circle isobar lines increasing in number. This is why when you listen to the shipping forecast they will say: "996mb and falling" or "996mb and rising". This indicates to mariners how the pressure system is developing and indicates deteriorating or improving weather.

How To Use
Razorfish

Sharpen your bait knowledge with this easy-to-follow guide.

Razorfish get their name because they look similar to the old-fashioned cut-throat razors. There are two types. The common razorfish is the larger of the two, growing up to 12 inches long and has a fairly straight shell. The smaller sword razorfish has a curved shell and only grows to about six inches.

They live along the low-water line and the beds can extend way out to sea in depths up to 100 feet. They prefer to live in fine, firmly packed sand rather than coarse sand that is continually moving. You can collect them on low spring tides by either digging with a fork – hard work – or with a container of salt or a salt-and-water mix.

They're quite easy to find once you get the hang of it. Simply look for little key-shaped holes in the sand, pour the salty water in and wait for the razor to emerge. When an inch or two of the shell appears take a firm hold and pull gently until it releases its grip. If you pull too fast you'll lose the foot or be left with an

Razorfish – fresh or frozen – are good bait for many species.

empty shell.

Razorfish can be collected all year round but will burrow deeper during frosty spells, as worms and other marine creatures do, to avoid the cold.

They are an excellent bait for many species, such as cod, bass, bream and flatfish, and can be used whole, in bunches or smaller pieces in a cocktail with worms and can be frozen down for future sessions.

How To Bait Up With Razorfish…

Open the shell and slide the flesh out with your finger.

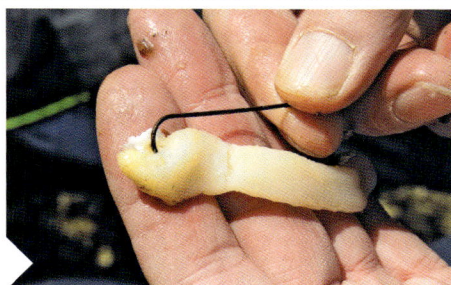

Thread the hook through the foot as if it were a worm.

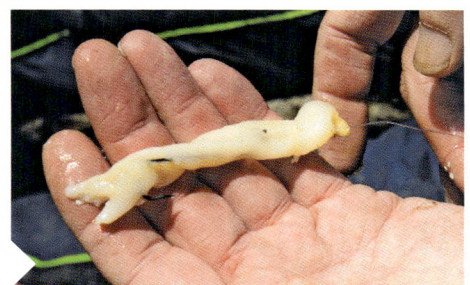

Once you've threaded it on the hook, make sure the hook point is showing.

Bind it securely to the hook with fine elastic.

Once bound on, it can be cast a long way and will withstand small fish nibbling at it.

It can also be used to make up juicy cocktails with rag and crab.

Find The Features,
Find The Fish

To get the very best out of your fishing it pays to know the ground you're fishing over. Barney Wright explains rough-ground feature finding…

Rough ground offers the very best food-finding opportunity for fish. Rocks and boulders are full of hidey holes where a variety of crabs, small fish and shellfish can live with some security. This is a permanently filled larder, where fish of many species can be caught.

But even within this food-filled feature, there are small areas that produce by far the best numbers of fish.

Identifying these specific areas and why they fish so well is essential to making the most of any rough-ground mark.

SHALLOW ROUGH-GROUND BEACHES

Shallow rough ground is relatively easy to read because much of the ground features, within casting distance, will be exposed on the bigger spring tides. A walk on the beach over a low-water spring tide will show you much of what you will be fishing into when the tide starts to flood back.

Try to look at the ground and identify obvious routes the fish will use to work their way inshore.

Causeways or rocky promontories and reefs running straight out to sea are prime routes. Fish will run the full length of such structure, working around the base of the rocks hoping to flush out small fish and crabs. During a full flood and ebb tide numbers of fish can be expected to feed along the base of the structure facing directly

Look at the shoreline rocks and you can pretty much guarantee that the underwater structure will be the same.

A Harsh and bumpy

B Levelish with lots of cracks and crannies

into the tide. Any food washed along by the tide will collect here and can be easy pickings for fish.

Fish swim inwards on the flood, but obviously swim along the structure in an offshore direction during the ebb, requiring a change of side. This also means, generally speaking, that short casts will be most effective on the flood, but on the ebb the fish tend to be further out, wary of being cut off by the receding tide, so longer casts are needed.

Also look for deeper gullies and gutters that run in towards the beach. These are excellent fish-holding features, as any northeast rock cod angler worth his salt will tell you – the deeper gullies and gutters are used by the fish time and again as routes into the feeding grounds. But these gutters, being deeper, also trap food that's washed out by the tide flow and trundled along until it falls into the gutter. Bass and cod anglers especially need to identify these areas, as they are real hotspots for ambushing fish.

GET DOWN!
During low water, from the low-water line looking back up the beach, but more so from the high tide line looking seaward, get down on your hands and knees and look at the incline of the beach. If you do this carefully you will realise that some areas are not of an even depth, with slightly deeper areas among more even ground. The same principle works here – waterborne food will collect in the deeper sections and these are hotspots.

PRECISE
You can look at this in micro-form too. While walking the rough ground backwards and forwards over a specific length, look for and pinpoint definite

depressions in flatter ground. These may be only the size of a dining table. Good indicators are pools of standing water among dry ground. Bass and cod always come to these to check if any food has been washed in and held there when the tide floods in.

This is so precise for depth of water and tide run that bass and cod can be predicted to visit that exact depression at a specific time of tide. If you don't get a bite within that anticipated five to 10-minute period, then it's likely the fish aren't there at all. Some anglers find this hard to understand, but bass and cod specialists, once they have learnt their patch, can be that precise on exactly when and where to fish.

UNDER COVER

If the ground you want to fish doesn't expose with the tide, then look at low water for weed beds, which show on a calmish surface as shimmering water. Sometimes the tops of the weed beds will show sticking up on the surface too. Always fish to the downtide side of these for the best results.

Also read the surf pattern. Close-in surf between waves breaking further out denotes deeper water and is the place to fish.

BOILING

Pick a big tide and sit on the rocks watching the surface of the sea for up to 100 yards out. Note areas where the water boils up – uptide of these there will be

Boulders

Make a note of big boulders, and especially areas where numerous boulders bigger than the average are positioned, that sit among generally more even ground. If you look at the base of these you will see around the underside that the ground has been washed out and dished. As food gets pushed along by the tide it comes to rest in the washout around the base of these boulders, and fish come to these markers consistently tide after tide.

Fish will also visit small patches of clean shingle and sand in among areas of boulders. Small flatfish and sandeels will live here and bass sweep across these on the off-chance of scaring up an easy meal.

Large boulders hold fish on the downtide side.

Four Typical Rough-Ground Fish-Holding Areas

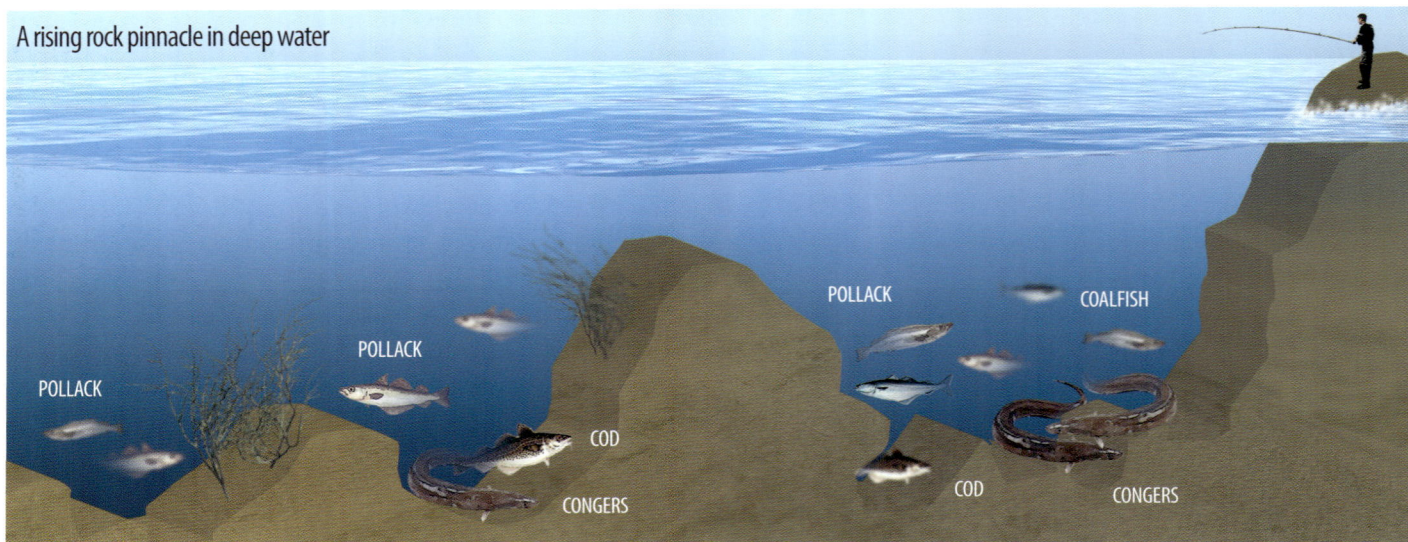

A rising rock pinnacle in deep water

POLLACK
POLLACK
POLLACK
POLLACK
COALFISH
COD
CONGERS
COD
CONGERS

Where the congers and huss will be when fishing off a rock ledge

BULL HUSS
BULL HUSS
CONGERS

Deep-Water Rock Ledges

Deep-water rock ledges and casting into rough ground are the hardest marks of all to find fish-holding features on. Depths can vary from 40 to more than 100 feet, depending on which part of the country you're fishing in.

The first thing to do is to stand on the mark you have chosen and look to either side at the cliffs, rocks and general geography and see how it falls into the sea. It's often the case that what you can see above the water continues down under the water. Short casts will put you in among underwater rock ledges, much like what you're standing on, but equally may place baits onto steep-shelving flat rock.

Rockies

Any inlets of water between rocks that cut deep into the cliff face are top marks for wrasse – also called 'rockies' for obvious reasons. Wrasse are territorial and will work along and around these inlets or fissures, constantly looking for food. Wrasse will also be right under your feet at the base of vertical rock ledges and around uprising boulders on the sea bed running out from the rock ledge.

This fishing will mean literally dropping the bait in at your feet, using a light lead, and letting the wash of the tide move the bait naturally.

Look for reefs of rock running out from the cliffs. Where these drop into deep water you will find pollack in the mid-water column, but wrasse down the sides, with congers, huss, ling and cod around the base.

underwater structures that cause the tide to boil the water. This is a good place to put a bait or lure as it will be a hard, uprising structure that will hold fish. You may need to make searching casts to find this structure initially.

Vertical or near-vertical ledges will see fish run along the base of them, while congers and huss will make their homes here to intercept passing prey. Often these vertical ledges have collapsed at some stage and their bases will be covered in an avalanche of broken boulders, providing homes for bigger

predators such as ling.

Rising rock pinnacles are great features to locate. These can be just a few feet high, or maybe 40 feet or more in very deep water. Around their base will be huss, congers, cod and ling. Higher up around overhanging rock, and on the downtide side of the pinnacle in midwater, will be pollack and coalfish. Remember that round fish, such as pollack and coalies, will change sides with the tide flow, preferring the downtide side, using the passing tide to bring prey fish to them. Anglers keen on spinning for pollack need to know this.

BAYS

If you see a small bay, and by small we mean nothing more than 100 yards across, then

Where wrasse will be when fishing off a rock ledge

WRASSE

WRASSE

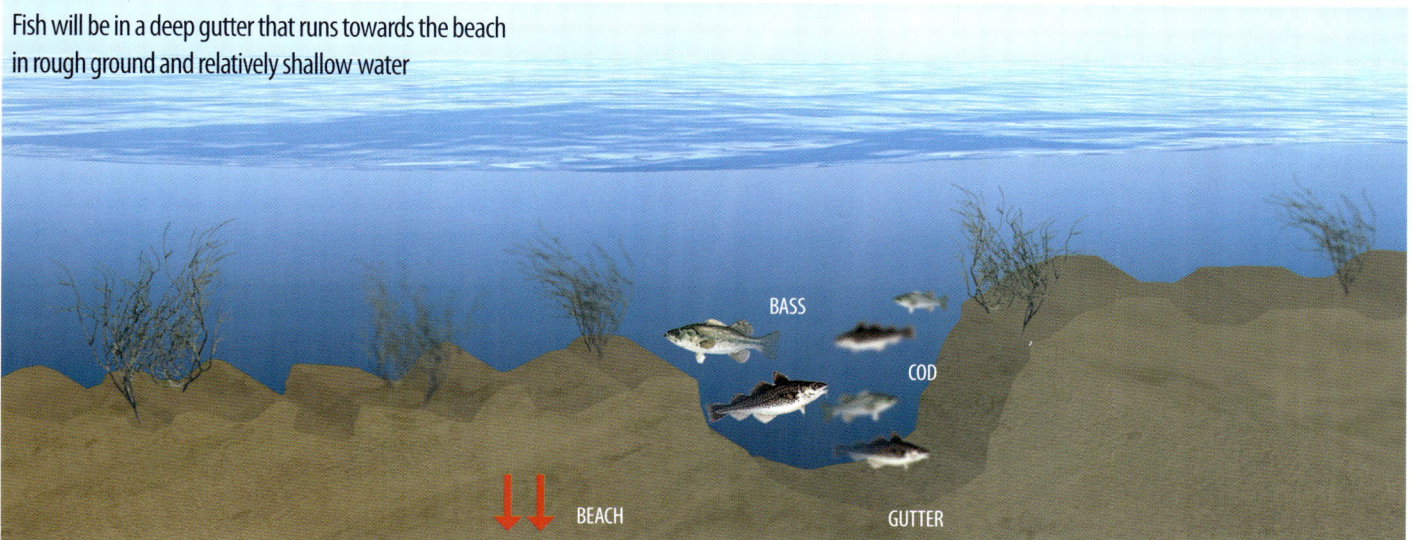

Fish will be in a deep gutter that runs towards the beach in rough ground and relatively shallow water

BASS

COD

BEACH

GUTTER

The tide will race through channels where a small island is near the shore. Mackerel love these areas!

The wrasse is a classic rock-dwelling species.

Structure beneath the surface will show as disturbed or 'boiling' water on the surface.

Rocky ground will hold lots of food when the tide covers it.

cast baits into the mouth of it where you judge the edge of the passing tide is. These are good fish-holding spots, with congers, huss, small ling and smaller species all likely, but you must be on the divide line of the flowing tide.

A quick learning curve can be achieved by putting each additional cast out in a wide arc shape in front of you. Do this at say 30, 50, 70 yards, and also up to as far as you can cast. Space each cast 10 feet apart. If you make a mental note you will come to identify where there are vertical ledges, rising rock pinnacles, big boulders and cleaner ground.

You will also learn that a cast within a few feet of a certain specific area will produce three-bearded rockling, another mark a conger, another a huss, and so on. Fish are that specific in exactly what type of ground feature they prefer to live and feed on. This is why fish are all shapes and sizes, so they can capitalise on different ground to feed at all available food opportunities.

POLLACK

Pollack anglers using lures should also use the casting in an arc technique to locate fish. By doing this you will come across small rock pinnacles and bigger patches of boulders where you seem to take fish after fish, with ground around it producing nothing. This is no coincidence. Pollack tend to form small shoals around suitable structure and, where you get one fish, you will get another.

A good place for mackerel and pollack is in the tide run between the shore cliffs and a small island situated just out from the cliffs, providing the water is deep. Mackerel like the fast tide, and the pollack sit underneath the mackerel, both feeding on sandeel shoals that are pushed through this bottleneck by the tide.

Conclusion

Too many anglers shy away from rough ground, being frightened of losing tackle and leads. Yet rough ground will yield far greater returns of fish, plus produce much bigger fish, generally, than any other type of ground feature.

To get the very best from rough ground you need to first conquer your fear of tackle losses, and fish rigs that reduce the loss to snags. The second and most important step is to learn to see and find the features described in this article. It takes time to learn rough-ground marks, but the rewards are immense!

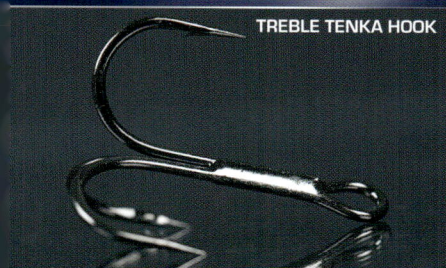

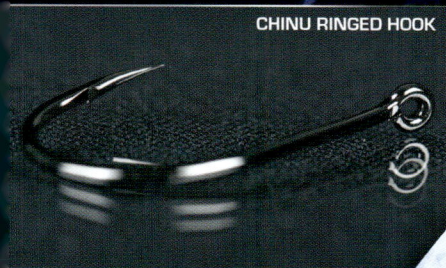

The Bomber Rig

Roger Mortimore reveals some of the best sea angling traces for you to use.

A bomber rig will blow all other traces out of the water when it comes to casting small baits to maximum range. Many anglers believe that the rig was spawned from the original one-hook paternoster, but this is not the case. It was developed by several anglers realising the effectiveness of having two hooks fishing close together, along with the advantage of having both a long and short hooklength to vary bait presentation. Nobody can prove who the original instigator was, although many like to lay claim to it!

The rig is said to be a matchman's 'banker' rig at long range, when all else fails. The bomber is designed to achieve maximum range when using two small baits. This is due to its streamlined nature, with both baits being clipped, side by side, into the Impact Shield and flying through the dead air behind the shield to minimise the wind resistance.

Top tips

When retrieving a bomber trace with no fish on, never reel in too quickly because the snoods can become tangled, especially as you draw it through the surf.

If using single hooks on the snoods, ensure that you use bait stops to prevent the bait from blowing back up the snood, otherwise this will dramatically cut casting distance and damage the bait.

You can also use Impact Leads instead of Impact Shields. If you choose to fish at extreme range, Impact Leads will be more effective.

When setting the hooks in the Impact Shield, I prefer to put the bigger bait in first followed by the smaller one. Occasionally, if placing the smaller bait in the shield first, it can fail to eject from the shield's retaining arm.

Build Sequence

Begin with 30 inches of 60lb or 80lb rig-body mono and tie a Gemini lead link to one end.

Slide on a Breakaway Impact Shield followed by a 3mm bead and crimp. Leave around one and a half inches for the shield to slide in; this will avoid hook-snood stretch during the cast.

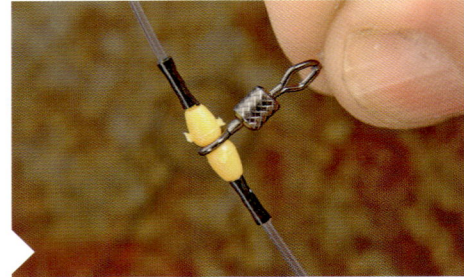

Slide on a rig crimp, a 3mm rig bead, a size 10 rolling swivel, another bead and a crimp. Now repeat the sequence so that you have two sets of components ready for fixing to the rig body. Finish off the main rig body by tying on a size 4 rolling swivel.

Tie 12 inches of 25lb fluorocarbon line to the lower hook-snood swivel.

Slide on a rubber rig stop and a sequin, then finish with a size 2 Aberdeen hook for smaller species, or a 1/0 Viking hook for bigger fish. Place the hook in the Impact Shield and slide the lowest snood crimp up the rig until the snood line comes just tight. Hold everything firm and crimp the trace swivel in position.

The top hook trace needs to be around 24 inches long with a stop and sequin threaded on. This is, again, positioned by placing the hook in the Impact Shield, sliding the swivel and crimp assembly up the line until the trace comes tight. Crimp this in place. Both hooks will sit in the Impact Shield for casting, but release when the lead hits the water.

How It Works

The bomber rig is traditionally chosen for fishing at medium to long range, but mostly long. It has the ability to present two different baits relatively close together to give single fish a choice, but also the two different baits can be used to tempt different types of fish. For example, you could have a mackerel strip for dogfish and whiting on one hook, and worm bait for flatfish on the other. This is why the rig is often referred to as the matchman's 'banker' rig, because it multiplies your chances of fish when you can only fish the one rig and need to be at maximum range.

Another benefit of this rig is that the shorter, lower hook trace will fish bait hard on the sea bed, and will target bottom feeders, such as flatfish. The top, longer trace will flutter and swing in the tide giving a more natural form of presentation and target fish feeding and swimming just up off the sea bed.

Some anglers choose to use the bomber rig with a small size 4 or 2 Aberdeen hook on the bottom hook trace for the smaller fish. They then go for a single 2/0 or 3/0 Viking pattern on the longer, top trace, fishing bigger worm or crab baits to target bass, cod and the like to cover their options.

When fishing at long range in shallow surf conditions, even at night, I prefer to make the hook traces from fluorocarbon line, as it is stiffer than mono. This helps avoid any chance of the two hook traces tangling as the surf lifts over the rig and tumbles them around. In calm seas you can switch to softer and lighter clear monofilament lines to increase the natural movement of the baits.

The rubber rig stop and sequin act as a bait stop, preventing the bait from being blown back up the snood during a powerful cast due to air pressure. You can substitute the sequin for two or three 5mm attractor beads in clear water. This can increase your chances of plaice and other flatfish. Alternatively, at night, replace the sequin with a couple of small luminous beads to advertise the bait visually to hunting fish.

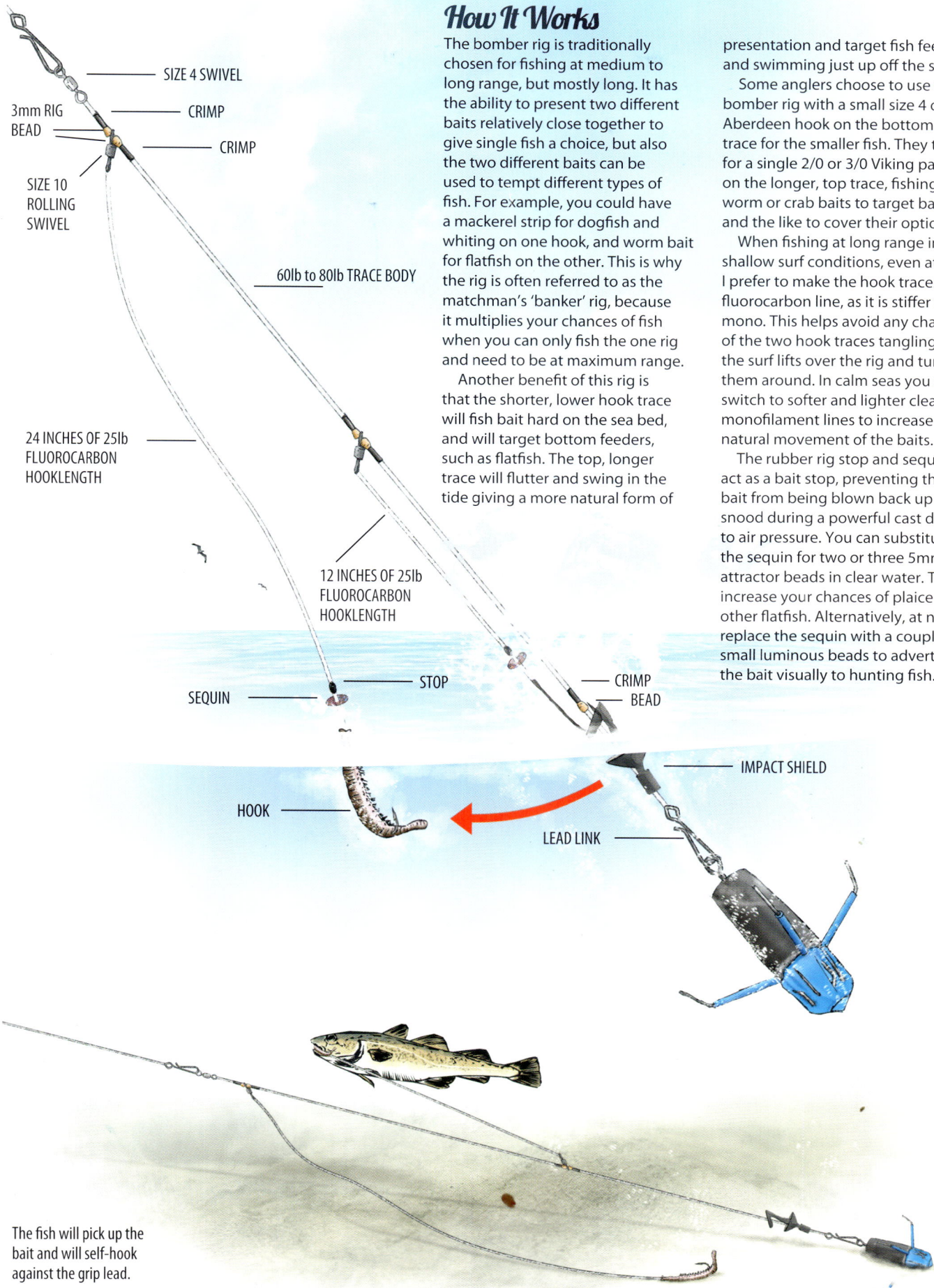

SIZE 4 SWIVEL

CRIMP

3mm RIG BEAD

CRIMP

SIZE 10 ROLLING SWIVEL

60lb to 80lb TRACE BODY

24 INCHES OF 25lb FLUOROCARBON HOOKLENGTH

12 INCHES OF 25lb FLUOROCARBON HOOKLENGTH

SEQUIN

STOP

CRIMP BEAD

HOOK

IMPACT SHIELD

LEAD LINK

The fish will pick up the bait and will self-hook against the grip lead.

The Spider-Hitch Shockleader Knot

Never worry about weak leader knots ever again, as we show you how to tie one of the strongest knots available.

t's not unusual for the leader knot to be the weakest link in your setup. This is often because the running line becomes crushed and stressed as a standard leader knot is formed – often reducing the line's breaking strain by 50 per cent! This means that if you're using 15lb running line, you now have, in effect, only 7$\frac{1}{2}$lb of pulling power before the line breaks. This is a complete disaster and will regularly result in lost gear as well as your entire leader length.

This is where the spider-hitch leader knot comes into its own because, if tied correctly, it is as close to 100 per cent strength as a leader knot can be. A strong knot will ensure that you don't lose fish, tackle or your temper, and will result in more time spent fishing and less time retying leaders!

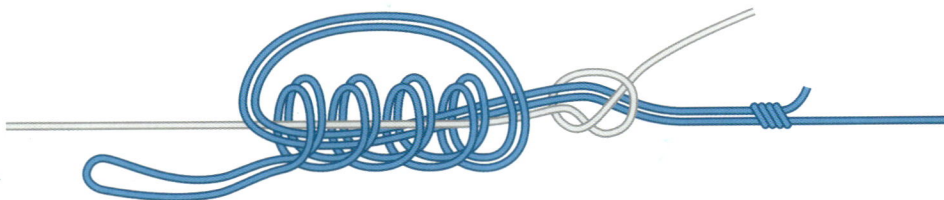

Top tips

When attaching the leader, use saliva on the running-line loop to help keep even lengths on the hitch.

Never use more than four turns when forming the uni knot because this pinches and weakens it.

To prevent line burn, use saliva as a lubricant whenever you create knots.

Try to keep the spider-hitch and overhand leader knot as close together as possible when forming the knot. You can achieve this by making the smallest loop possible when tying the uni knot.

How To Tie The Spider-Hitch Knot

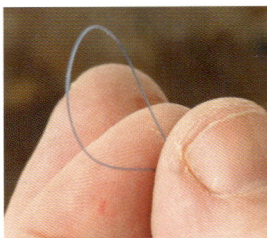

Form a 12in loop in the running line.

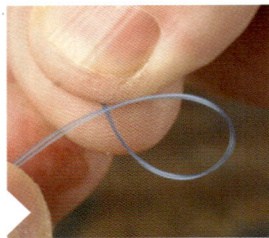

Make a small loop on top of your index finger, as shown, and grip tight.

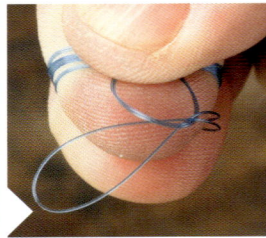

Wind the large loop around your finger four times and pass through the small loop.

Moisten with saliva then slowly pull the tag loop tight and the loops will come off one at a time.

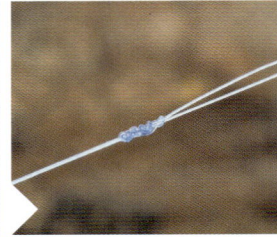

Push the coils together, then slowly pull tight with steady pressure.

How To Attach The Spider To The Leader

Form an overhand knot in the leader and pass the spider loop through about an inch or so, then tighten fully.

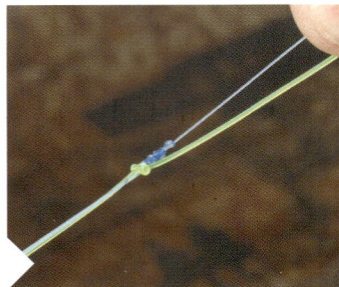

Lubricate the running line and slide the two knots together.

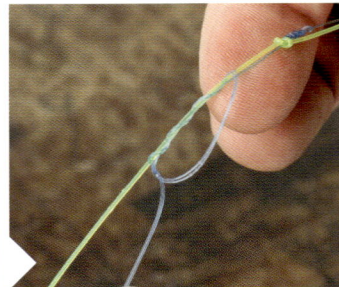

Create the smallest uni knot you can by using four turns and lubricate.

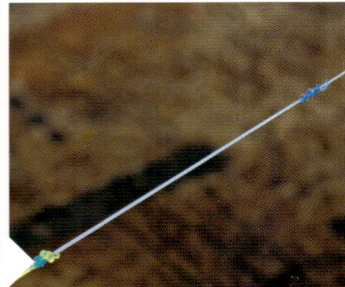

Push the coils together and tighten by applying steady pressure on both the leader line and running line. Trim the tags and that's it – done!

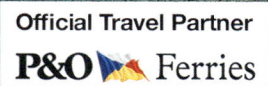

A Golden Grey Day

Mike Thrussell spends a day on the 'GGs' and comes away a winner.

Golden grey mullet, or GGs as they're commonly known, are hard-fighting fish and can be differentiated from other mullet by a gold spot on the gill cover. Their sporting prowess has been likened to that of the legendary bonefish, and if you fancy targeting them the best spot in the UK is probably Llangennith Beach on the Gower Peninsula, in South Wales.

They show all along this beach so there are no real hotspots, and don't be put off by surfers in the water in front of you – the greys certainly aren't! The first thing you find out about GGs is that they can literally be right at your feet in the nearest surf tables, so resist the urge to cast too far. If you wade out for them they will, on occasions, swim around you and be so close you could pick one up – that is if you were fast enough! However, despite their boldness, I'd never caught a golden grey mullet and was desperate to do so.

My long-time fishing buddy Colin Albert, from Cardiff, was in the same position and also wanted to add a golden grey to his species list. So, back in June 2009 we took a look at our diaries and found the one single day in September that we might be able to get together for a bash at the golden mullet.

Now, we all remember how bad the summer weather proved to be and, right up to two days before our trip, the wind was howling and the rain was pouring and there was flooding in parts of Wales. I was due some luck, however, and when we met up on the Gower, even though it was still blowing and raining up in North Wales as I left, the wind was non-existent and light cloud was just hiding the sun.

The tide was still ebbing but the surf tables had lost the wildness brought on by the recent winds and now a steady, even surf with long, flat tables was pushing ashore. The sea still carried some colour but was trying to clear and, best of all, there was no weed!

TACKLE

My aim was to fish as light as possible. I opted for an 11ft rod with a supple tip, but with some backbone in the mid-section and butt. I matched it to a Penn Sargus 4000 fixed-spool reel loaded with 12lb braid, then added an 8ft leader of 15lb fluorocarbon line just to hide the braid from the feeding fish.

Most anglers choose a single-hook sliding-leger rig, but Colin and I decided that, with colour in the water, a lot of scent would give us an advantage. We both opted for two-hook rigs – mine being made from 25lb fluorocarbon bodies using neoprene-tubing sliding stops to hold small, clear beads and the hook swivel in place. My hook snoods were 12lb fluorocarbon and 15 inches long, ending in a Kamasan B940 Aberdeen size 6 hook – one was positioned tight behind the lead clip and the other 30 inches away, just below the connector swivel. The aim was to make the rigs as inconspicuous to the fish as possible.

We'd also discussed whether to use a swimfeeder to increase the scent value and had come armed with a feeder mix of bran and mashed-up fish oils, plus a pack of halibut pellets. Colin decided to use the feeder but I chose to stick with a plain rig to give the bait more freedom in the tide.

You're constantly on the move as the beach

34

Maddies, or 'harbour rag', are the top bait for golden grey mullet.

necessarily so. We baited up with big bunches of maddies for maximum scent. Here's how…

HOW TO FISH

We chose light, ½oz flat watch leads to give us just enough weight to cast and to lightly hold bottom, yet allowing the lead to wash sideways with the current occasionally to give a natural presentation. One good way of standing to aid bite detection is to hold the rod across the body with the rod tip low to the water against a tight line. This is the one I use myself, often when bass fishing in the surf because you receive instant notification of a bite.

On the day, though, I found that facing the water and holding the rod at a 45° angle proved far more effective, plus the rising angle of the line gave the higher, second hook-trace bait more life and movement as the surf washed it around. It was interesting that those holding their rods low caught the bulk of their fish on the bottom hook, whereas I caught mine roughly equal on both hooks, simply due to the rising angle of the line.

FISH SPOTTING

Golden grey mullet are real surf dwellers and use the rolling surf tables to their advantage. The surf tables dig the sand out, exposing lots of small marine life that the mullet feed on. Often these fish are in just calf-deep water… and that's not an exaggeration.

When you're stood in the edge of the surf, wear polarising sunglasses

and look carefully in the flat water just behind the white surf line. If the GGs are there you'll see them with their tails out of the water doing a damn fine impression of bonefish as they feed head down.

You'll also see small and large shoals of them working along the surf-table line, splashing on the surface – rolling and turning as they feed. Try to anticipate where they're going and cast there. Don't cast directly into them because this can spook the fish.

ON THE DAY

The tides were falling away after reasonably high springers and it was two hours before low water. We weren't expecting much action because we'd heard that low water and the first hour of the flood were the best time.

On my second cast I was standing in the surf taking in the view of Worm's Head out to the left. My rod was at a 45° angle and held comfortably in one hand with the butt resting on my upper thigh. The next second there was a series of rapid-fire bangs on the rod tip, which then pulled hard over and the hook set into something that fought in a very unfamiliar way.

This fish tried to run parallel with the surf then turned and bored back into the white water. It even tried to broach and twist on the surf. Keeping the rod low and to the left, the fish was forced to turn and, as it headed for the sea and came side on to me, I knew I'd got my first golden grey mullet. It fought harder than a 3lb bass yet weighed in at just 1lb 5oz. What a start!

Keen to see Colin also achieve his goal,

is flat and the tide ebbs and floods fast. I had to use a big tackle box as I had my cameras with me. Colin, however, wisely chose to keep things as simple as possible and used a supported boilie bag screwed to his rod rest to keep his immediate gear close and to allow for instant access and full manoeuvrability. It also speeds up the fishing as everything is to hand!

BAIT

The best bait for golden greys at Llangennith is maddie rag. You can catch on small king rag, I'm told, but the maddies are must-have bait.

Some anglers make the mistake of thinking that GGs, being smallish fish, like a single maddie on a small hook – well, not

Local angler Julian Blarney with a cracking GG close to 3lb.

How To
Make A GG Bait

Thread one largish maddie onto the point of the hook and up onto the hook shank, leaving a little of the tail to hang free.
Slide two more maddies onto the shank, again leaving the tails to hang free.
Add three or four more maddies by just hooking them by the head onto the hook point to secure them, leaving their longish tails to flutter free in the tide.
This bunching effect proves deadly for the fish when in slightly coloured water as it gives a greater scent lane.

Mike lifts out his first-ever GG!

Flounders will often show during sessions for golden greys.

I kept a sly eye on him, and saw his rod go upwards to rapid rattles on the rod tip. He was using a light spinning rod and the tip buckled over to the weight of the fish. This mullet also ran up and down the surf, turning for the sea several times and fighting to the last second. I knew it was another GG and, as he slid it up on the sand, we exchanged wide smiles of satisfaction.

The fishing eased off over low water but I sneaked out a decent flounder – again on maddies and almost at my feet – and Colin took a lesser weever. We had surfers out in front of us and I looked at their bare feet and the weever's poisonous dorsal fin and shuddered at the thought!

Four local anglers then turned up and mentioned that there had been a few caught over the past couple of weeks but that the fishing had been patchy. One of these lads had the next mullet, about an hour after the tide turned, then Colin was in again with his second GG and I cursed as I lost a fish after playing it almost to the shore.

On the second hour of the flood you could occasionally see the mullet in the surf tables topping and waving their tails at you, but the shoals were infrequent. Then, as the incoming tide quickened, the fish really started to feed.

Colin had another small fish around the 1lb mark, followed by a bass. I was lagging behind now, but then reacted quickly to a powerful bite that saw me into another golden grey, which again whacked the rod more than a fish three times its size.

I'd got the flow of the fishing now and was really concentrating on keeping fresh baits out there. I'd also swapped over to a heavier lead to stay in better contact with the baits as the tide speeded up. Noticing that the activity tight in had ceased, I started putting my baits about 25 to 30 yards out.

I missed a bite almost as the bait hit the water, then rebaited and straightaway hooked into a better fish around 1½lb. One of the local lads to the right, Julian Blamey, shouted over to me that he'd got a cracker.

A Golden Grey Day

How To Get There

Leave the M4 at Junction 47 taking the A483, then bear right onto the B4295 for Gowerton. At Llanrhidian follow the signposts for Llangennith. We accessed the beach through the caravan site at Hillend, which costs just £3 for the day with safe parking close to the beach.

A swimfeeder packed with goodies is Colin Albert's choice instead of a lead.

It was too, and by the looks of it would have been close to 3lb – not far off the Welsh record! What a cracking fish.

I was flying now and over the next 25 minutes landed two more fish around the 1lb to 1½lb mark. Colin added another GG and a bass.

SPECIMEN TIME...

I was really looking to catch a golden grey over 2lb. This is a big fish for the species because most UK specimen weights for the fish are classed as 1½lb. This is also the Irish specimen size and I have the utmost respect for the Irish list when it comes to sizing fish accurately.

It crossed my mind that any bigger fish would likely be just that bit further out where the second wave was curling over with a deeper water table behind it. I dropped the baits there, raised the rod to a 45° angle and stood like a statue, waiting for the bite with real confidence.

The bite came five minutes later and I didn't feel the rattles that I'd had before, but a gentle tap – then I felt the lead slide

Colin is also no longer a GG virgin!

away to the right. I struck and the fish pretty much pulled the rod out of my hand. It was powerful and stayed out in the surf, only begrudgingly giving up a few feet of line at a time, then turning seawards and taking it back again. It made repeated turns and outward runs back out into the surf, but gradually I got it closer. When it felt the final surf table shallowing it went hard over to the right and actually took about 10 yards of line off the reel clutch, which was set slightly light now to allow for this.

It made one final parallel run then, still splashing its tail on the surface, I used a surf table to beach the fish. This was much bigger than I'd had before but I still hesitated that it would make 2lb. Colin weighed it for me at 2lb 1oz exactly – well over specimen weight!

We shared 11 GGs between us, plus the flounder, two bass and the weever. We'd both achieved an ambition in catching our first golden grey mullet, and had learnt a heck of a lot too.

38

Dig Your Own
Harbour Rag

Get the garden fork out and keep those pennies in your pocket.

Lively maddies are a great bait for many species.

Harbour rag, or 'maddies' as they're often called, are a very effective bait for many species, especially flatfish like flounders and sole. Like their bigger cousin, the king rag, they prefer to live in muddy estuaries but maddies can be found just below the high-water mark. All you need are wellies, a bucket and a normal garden fork as they can be found just a few inches down.

Digging maddies is a messy business but well worth the effort as you can save yourself a lot of cash by collecting your own bait. You can find out if they're present just by walking over the ground, so start digging if you see masses of tiny spurts of water.

Top match angler Alan Jeffery uses a riddle or colander in the top of his bucket and, as he digs, he puts the worms and any mud on top of the riddle. The worms will wriggle through, leaving the mud behind – clever eh!

Another tip is to back-fill where you've been digging as you'll find the previously dug area has attracted a lot more worms when you return a week or two later.

Alan also advises washing the worms on site in clean seawater, and you'll need to take some water home in a clean container too. They can be stored in cat-litter trays in an inch or so of water and kept in a fridge, but make sure the temperature of the water matches the temperature you dug them in because any sudden change can kill them. When they're stored this way, they should last a few weeks.

Digging Your Own...

The maddies' territory is often just off the saltings.

You'll soon know if you're digging in the right area as there will be maddies everywhere.

Once you've found them, use a riddle to separate the worms from the mud and...

... at the end of your dig you'll have plenty of lively maddies.

When you get home put 50 to 100 maddies in a shallow tray ready for storing.

Finally, keep the trays of worms in the fridge at the same temperature you dug them in.

The Albright Knot

This is the best way to join braided lines to monofilament.

The reason we need to join braid and mono lines is because braid has no stretch and a low abrasion resistance, so we counter this by attaching a mono leader to act as a shock absorber and rubbing line.

The problem is that braid and mono are very different in their properties and are particularly hard to join by using standard knots, since the braid can easily slip away from the mono – but the Albright is the solution to this. The main application for this knot is for boat fishing.

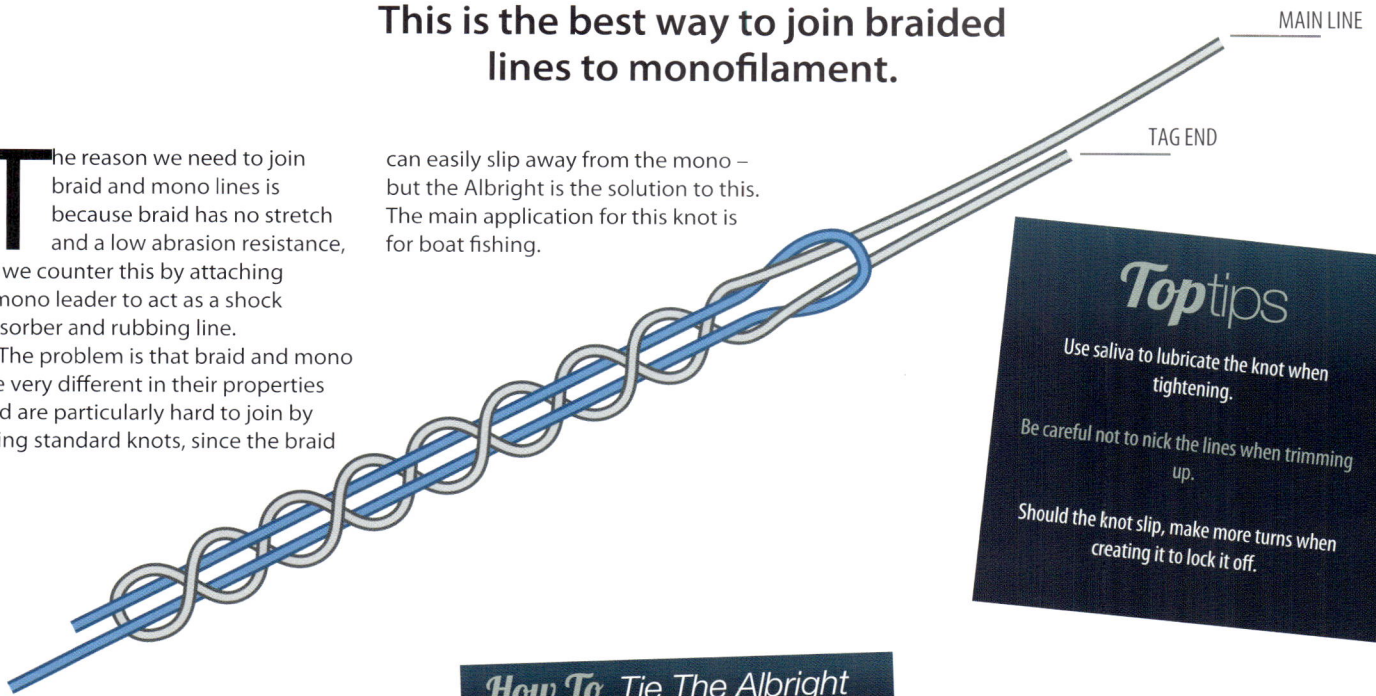

MAIN LINE

TAG END

Top tips

Use saliva to lubricate the knot when tightening.

Be careful not to nick the lines when trimming up.

Should the knot slip, make more turns when creating it to lock it off.

How To Tie The Albright

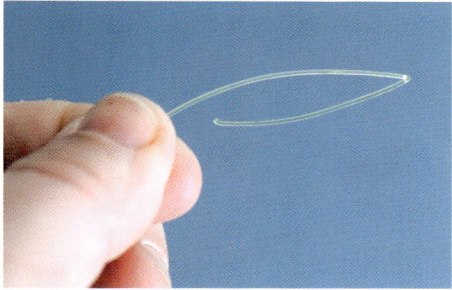

Form a loop in the monofilament – try to squeeze it to a rough point.

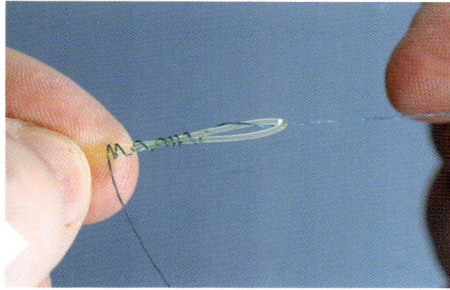

Pass the braid through the loop and make eight turns downward.

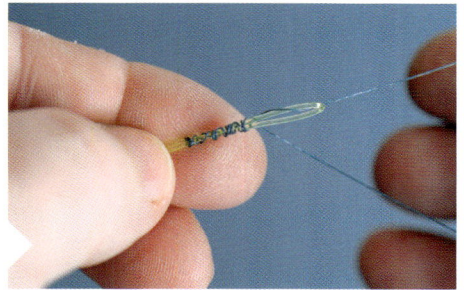

Now make another eight turns back up over the previous turns.

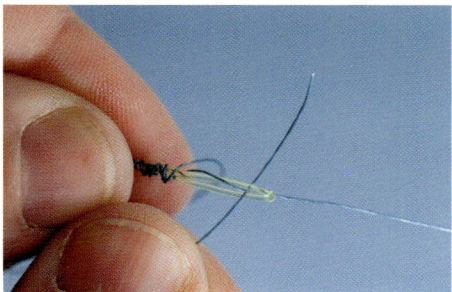

Pass the tag end out through the loop, the same way it came in.

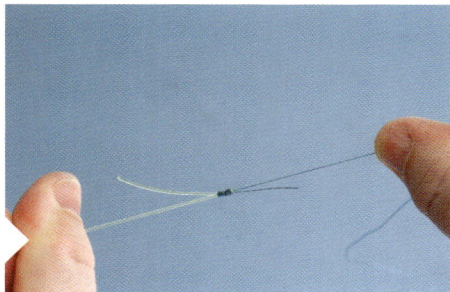

Slowly pull the coils up by pulling both the braid and the running line.

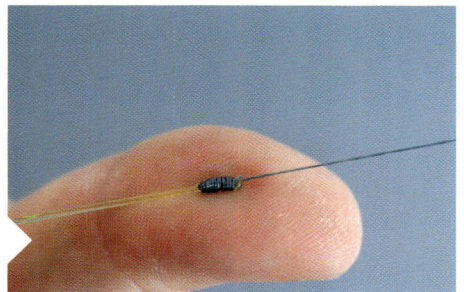

When the coils are bunching up nicely, pull just the running line while holding the mono leader until it's tightened. Trim the tags and that's it!

The Shore Three-Hook Reversible Flapper Rig

Stan Piecha reveals some of the best sea angling traces for you to use.

This rig is one of the most successful rigs, and a clone of the first three-hook flappers that became popular for both match and freelance fishing during the early 1970s.

Anglers often quote it as being the ultimate all-round rig, but it's actually the reversible flapper that offers the most versatile fishing. It is a rig that all anglers should have in their rig wallets when targeting general species.

How It Works

So why is the three-hook flapper design so successful? Firstly, it positions three hooks relatively close together, producing a wide and strong scent trail that fish can follow easily to find the baits.

You can use different baits on the different hooks to experiment on the day and see what bait, or bait combination, is most successful. This simple trial-and-error process will make a massive difference to your overall catch rate more often than not.

Secondly, and this is the key to this particular rig, is that the three hooks present baits differently. When fishing to a tight line,

the lower hook sits close to or on the sea bed and targets flatfish, the middle one has more movement in the tide and will take a variety of both round fish and flatfish, and the top hook has even more freedom and appeals mostly to round fish hunting just up off the sea bed, such as whiting and coalfish.

Also notice that the lengths of the hook traces vary. A common mistake is to make all the hook traces of an equal short length on three-hook rigs. When you're fishing to a tight line at close to medium range, this kind of rig cannot sit flat on the sea bed. This often results in fish only being caught on the bottom hook trace with the other higher-positioned hooks almost redundant because they are not in the fishes' feeding zone.

The rig described uses a longer top and middle trace; it's designed like this to keep the baits tighter to the sea bed and in the fishes' feeding zone when fishing at close to medium range – without the need to fish a slack line between the rod tip and lead weight. They also encourage more natural movement, which can increase the number of bites you receive. ▶

Build Sequence

Start with about 64 inches of 60lb clear mono, and tie on a SALT lead link at one end.

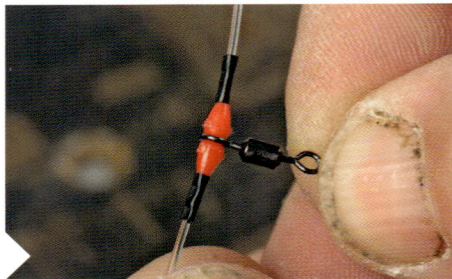

Slide on a rig crimp, a 3mm ovalised rig bead, a size 10 swivel, another rig bead and a crimp. Repeat this sequence to give you three full sets of crimps, beads and swivels. Leave these loose for now.

Complete the rig by tying on an inverted SALT lead link.

The first hook-trace swivel needs to be placed just one inch below the top SALT lead link. The middle swivel should be positioned exactly 17 inches below the top swivel, and the third again 17 inches down from the middle hook-trace swivel.

The top hook trace needs to be the longest at about 15 inches, the second hook trace should measure 13 inches, and the bottom hook trace will be the shortest at just 10 inches. Each hook trace should be made from 25lb mono or fluorocarbon and finished with a size 2 Kamasan B940 hook for general species.

However, when conditions are calm and you're fishing at close range, by fishing a tight line between the rod tip and lead weight, the top two hooks can be deliberately lifted up off the sea bed a little to lift the baits up periodically, as a surf table passes overhead, away from the sea bed, and target active swimmers such as whiting and coalfish.

Where the 'reversible' bit comes in is that by having a link at both ends of the rig body, you can literally turn this rig around. For instance, if all the fish are coming to the bottom hook, with the lower hook trace positioned well up above the lead, reverse the rig so that what was the top hook now fishes tight behind the lead, with the middle hook now positioned where the first one was before you reversed the rig around. This now puts two hooks in the feeding zone, giving you the chance to double your catches.

This versatility not only increases your catch rate, but also means that you need to carry fewer rigs, although you still have all the options available to you.

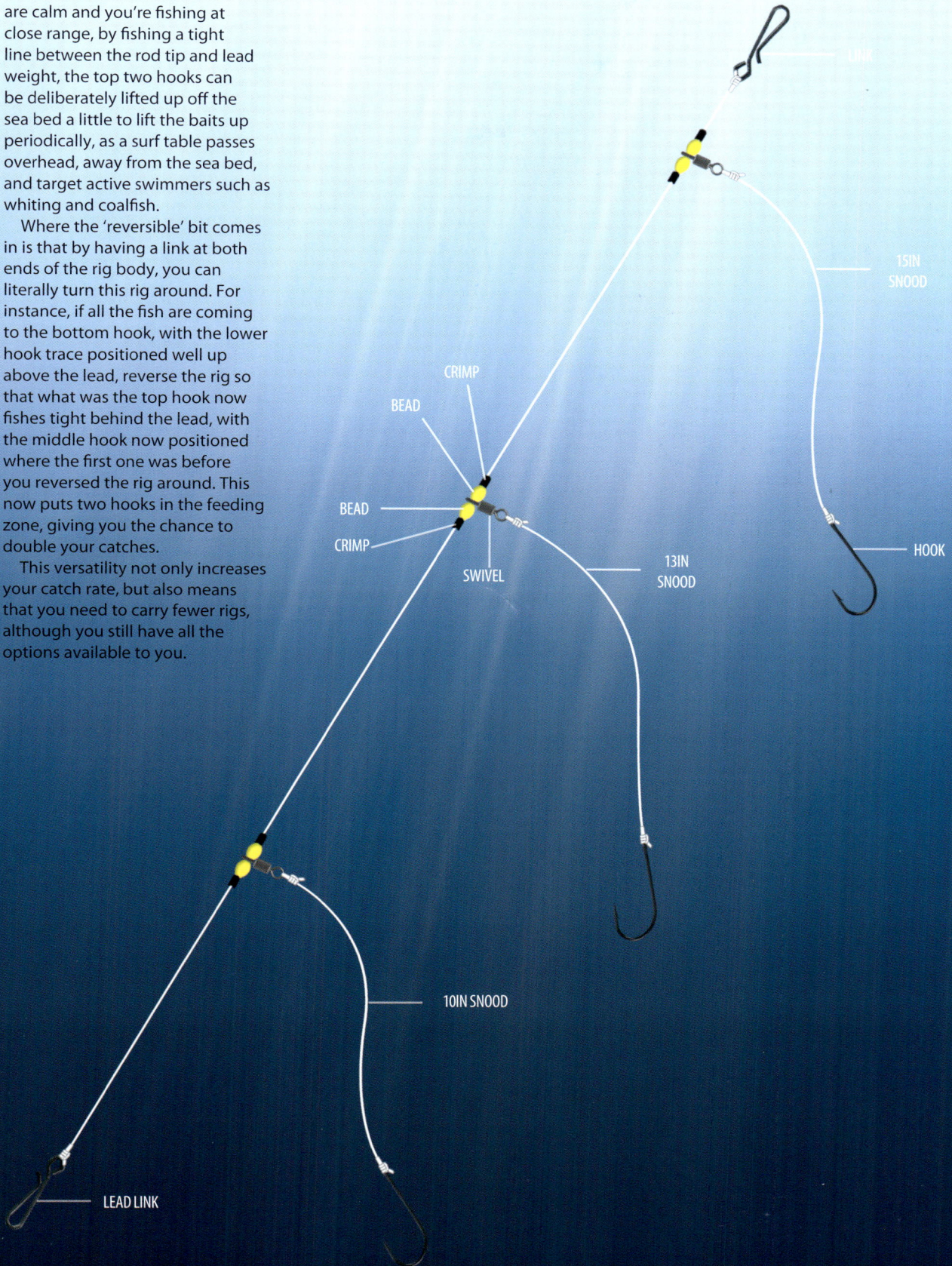

LINK

15IN SNOOD

CRIMP

BEAD

BEAD

CRIMP

SWIVEL

HOOK

13IN SNOOD

10IN SNOOD

LEAD LINK

Sky Mackerel

David Hall explains how Mother Nature affects our fishing…

Is there something fishy about this sky – or is it just a mackerel?

Many people will have heard of the phrase 'mackerel sky', but what does it mean and how does it help us in forecasting the weather?

Mackerel skies comprise cirrocumulus or altocumulus clouds. Cirrocumulus clouds are made up of highly super-cooled water droplets that quickly convert to ice crystals, or a mixture of both. These even-sized cloud particles can cause a halo or coronae of iridescence around the moon or sun, as they are thin and transparent in composition with little real density. They appear in regular waves with patches of blue sky showing through. They literally look like the scales of a mackerel, hence the name.

One of the sayings regarding weather associated with mackerel skies comes from the old mariners. It goes: "Mackerel sky, mackerel sky, never long wet and never long dry." Another is: "Mackerel skies and mare's tails make tall ships carry small sails." The sailors knew from experience that the appearance of a mackerel sky was the forerunner to potential stormy weather because it heralds a front moving in. In high winds sailing ships may need to minimise the amount of sail they carry, giving reference to the small sails. Small and white cirrocumulus clouds form at an altitude of about 17,000 to 30,000 feet and form ahead of incoming weather depressions and their associated frontal systems. Mackerel skies and mare's tails describe forms of cirrocumulus clouds and long strands of high cirrus clouds that forecast high-level winds and surface winds to come.

If a mackerel sky and mare's tail precede an approaching warm front, they will thicken and the winds will veer from a northwesterly direction into the southwest, and it's likely that the wind will freshen too as it backs anti-clockwise.

The general width of a warm front is around 500 kilometres, which is the rough distance working backwards from the edge of the first hazy clouds until you reach the rain belt. What this breaks down to is that when you see a mackerel sky, the rain is still 400 kilometres away and approaching. The front will move at about 50 kilometres per hour, so this tells us that the change in the weather will occur within roughly an eight-hour period – a handy thing to know!

Another saying related to mackerel skies is: "If there is a halo around the sun or moon, then we can expect rain quite soon." The halo around the sun or moon is caused by the refraction of light through the ice crystals that form the high cirrus clouds in front of an approaching weather front. The halo sometimes looks to carry a rainbow colour or prism effect – again, a noted sign of rain to come according to folklore.

If the mackerel sky is made up of larger and darker-coloured altocumulus clouds, these can suggest a short-term improvement, but rain will still arrive within 18 to 36 hours. Altocumulus clouds consist mostly of water droplets and typically form at altitudes of between 10,000 to 18,000 feet. If these grow into bigger, thicker clouds they can turn into a thunderstorm, which is often associated with a cold front.

People from past times often only had observation to forecast the weather by, but over time this proved highly accurate and even today the phrases passed down to teach people of those times have been proven to be as accurate as modern weather prediction!

Follow Your Piers

Words Barney Wright

Piers offer structure, deep water, strong tidal flow and comfortable fishing, and Deal Pier in Kent is a prime example. We join Chris Hajjar for a smoothhound session to remember.

P iers are ideal locations for all levels of angler. A novice can fish off a pier without the need for expensive gear and casting experience and still catch fish. A simple rod and reel will suffice and all he/she must do is lower a baited trace over the side... that's it! Fish will be all around the structure of the pier, feeding on the plentiful bounty provided by these features, such as fry, shellfish, crabs, prawns and suchlike.

The experienced anglers will know the 'hotspots' on the pier and also any features farther out to sea that can be reached by a good cast. This is the only time that the expert does better than the novice on a pier – but it doesn't take long for the novice to catch up by learning to cast safely and, by talking to the locals, where the best places are to fish.

Baiting Up With Peeler Crab

Completely remove all of the shell from the crab.

Using scissors, cut the crab about three-quarters of the way through.

Begin putting the crab on the hook by passing the hook through a leg socket.

Now weave the hook through the crab.

Use bait elastic to secure the crab to the hook.

The finished product – a perfectly presented smoothhound bait.

Barney Wright lifts a smoothhound over the pier railings for Roger Mortimore.

Angler Profile

Name Chris Hajjar
Occupation Electrician
Fave rod Daiwa 129
Fave reel Abu Mag Elite
Fave fish black bream and bass
Best fish 12lb bass
Fave venue Grenham Bay/Thannet Rocks.

HOMEWORK FIRST

I decided to pay a visit to Deal Pier in Kent where my intended target species were to be smoothhounds and thornback rays. Before I made the decision to go, I did the single most important thing that one should do before going on any trip, and this was to seek local knowledge as to how well the pier was fishing. Luckily my good friend Steve Allmark once owned Channel Angling, the tackle shop at the entrance of the pier, and it was from him that I sought advice.

Steve was the 2004 World Shore Fishing Champion and is still a brilliant angler, and nobody knows Deal Pier better than him! He suggested that we get down soon because the water was coloured and, therefore, the hounds were in, as well as a few rays. But if the water clears up it could be a wasted trip. It's this kind of information that's pure gold, because, although there's never a guarantee to catch fish, we had the best chance of hooking into something and making the trip worthwhile.

Steve also informed me that we'd need peeler crab for the hounds and blueys for the rays. However, he said that the hounds were mostly being caught with velvet swimmer crabs, which did present a problem because we only had shore crabs and Steve had run out of velvets! But I thought that normal peelers would be fine... how on earth can a hound tell the difference between the two? I was in for quite a surprise!

TO THE RESCUE!

Luck was on our side, as a good mate of Steve's, Chris Hajjar, was going to join us for our session and he had some velvet swimmer crabs left over from the previous day's fishing. Although he only had half a dozen or so, if what Steve says is correct and the hounds are, indeed, not interested in shore crabs, then these few crabs could save the day.

ON THE PIER

There must have been 20 or more anglers waiting for the gate of the pier to open and, once it was, we all rushed through and made a beeline for our favoured fishing spots. This was quite warming; it's great to see keen anglers ready to enjoy a session by the sea. The fact that there are more fish in the sea now than there have been in a long time certainly goes a long way toward this!

We set up at the end of the pier on the left-hand side and, fortunately, the water was still coloured, so we had high hopes for the day. The wind was howling from a westerly direction, which meant that the water could clear at any time – so we wasted no time in getting our bait out.

The ground here is noted for a few snags, so a pulley rig was the ideal choice for this session. The peeler crabs I had weren't especially big, so I only used size 2/0 hooks in Pennel form. I could place a whole crab on these hooks without masking the points. Roger Mortimore was also with me and he adopted pretty much the same tactics, but he was intent on bagging a ray. Roger was using two rods, one set up for hounds and the other used bluey as bait, because the rays love it!

I baited up with shore crab and safely cast it to around 100 yards. Now, it may seem daft to cast out when you're already 300 metres out, but at that distance there's a ledge and some structure where the majority of the hounds tend to pass through. They can be caught much closer, but the better numbers are further out.

We all sent our bait out to a similar distance, but the main difference, so far, was that only Chris had velvet swimmer crab on. This would be the

Chris Hajjar shows off his first smoothhound of the day.

Building A Pulley Rig

Cut a 40in section of 80lb mono and tie on a clipped-down link.

Thread on a bead, a 100lb swivel and another bead.

Finish this part of the rig by tying on a 100lb swivel.

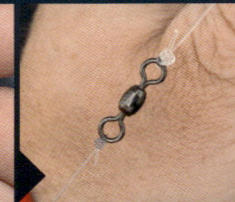

Now tie a 36in section of 40lb to 50lb mono for the snood to the 100lb swivel.

Use quality hooks in a size to match the bait. We used Sakuma Manta Extras in a 2/0.

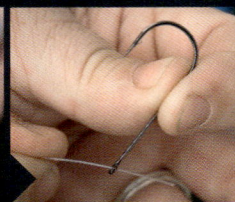

Pass the line through the top hook in this direction.

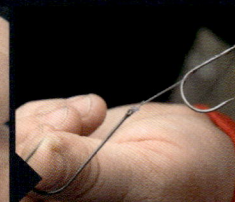

Finish off by tying on the bottom hook – job done!

Select a lead to suit the strength of the tide flow and bait.

Hold a dogfish as shown here. Their skin is abrasive and you could do yourself some serious damage holding them the wrong way.

Before placing the rod in its rest, loosen the drag so that the fish can take line when the rod is left unattended.

perfect test now to see if Steve was right and that the hounds were only munching the velvets.

FIRST FISH...

Steve's advice appeared to be spot on, as Chris was into a hound on his very first cast! I remember thinking: "Crikey! It's unusual to catch this quickly. We normally have to sweat it out for a while hoping the fish will show."

But that's the way it was, a fish was hooked and making its way towards the captor. Within a couple of minutes, a lovely starry smoothhound was lifted over the railings... result! This catch meant that I watched my rod tip even more closely, as did Roger, because we know that smoothies travel in packs and we were sure to have our own fish soon.

However, this wasn't the case and I was feeling somewhat disgruntled. Chris said: "Told you Barney, they're loving the velvets!" Chris offered me one, but I declined and decided to stick it out with shore crab as I was absolutely certain that I would catch a smoothhound on this bait.

VELVETS RULE

I made a few more casts and, after watching Chris catch a couple more, I was convinced that velvets must be the reason why he was catching where Roger and I were not. Eventually I took Chris up on his offer and eagerly popped it on the hooks. It could have only been a few minutes later before my rod tip was showing a typical 'nod nod' and then slack line.

Velvet swimmer crabs accounted for the smoothhounds caught.

49

This was definitely a hound. "Well I'll be a monkey's uncle," I thought!

It wasn't a particularly big fish, but it was nonetheless a smoothhound – I was made up. Roger soon followed suit and popped a velvet onto his hooks, which soon resulted in – yes, you've guessed it – a hound. This is when a big problem occurred. Both Roger and myself thought it unfair to continue using Chris's bait. We both decided that we would stick it out with normal crab and let Chris enjoy his day – he didn't mind because this meant he would definitely get his face in the magazine!

Roger and I were, nevertheless, happy because we had succeeded in our quest. Roger was still after a ray though, so he loaded both his rods with bluey to try and achieve his goal. Since I felt that shore crabs weren't working, I decided to have a play around the pier legs with a half bluey as bait to try for a bass. In the meantime, Chris continued to catch hounds – that was until he completely ran out of velvets!

JOB DONE!

We sat it out for quite some time; the tide was beginning to flood and water was shearing off. This was when it all went quiet, except for a few doggies, and the hounds seemed to vanish. We didn't give up, though, and persevered for another couple of hours, but in our hearts we knew that the session was over where hounds were concerned. Roger still hadn't managed to catch a ray and realised that he probably wasn't going to either on this trip – another time mate...

As the water cleared, Chris pulled out a little rod and popped some feathers onto it. I asked what he intended doing as I thought there were no mackerel here. He told me that he was after a couple of herring; I thought that he was off his trolley!

You could have called me what you like when, after a little perseverance, he managed to catch one. This would make perfect bait, but Chris had other ideas and was going to cook it up for a snack later on! Fair play to him, after all, they are delicious and healthy eating too.

About Deal Pier

This is the third pier to have been built on this spot, and is the only one in Britain to have been constructed after the Second World War. It was designed by Sir W Halcrow & Partners and was built entirely of reinforced concrete. The Duke of Edinburgh opened the pier on November 19th, 1957. It's 1,026 feet (311 metres) long, and has a three-tiered head containing a bar, café and lounge. This makes it ideal for the angler, as it has all the facilities that a beach in the middle of nowhere hasn't! There's also a tackle shop, Channel Angling, where you can buy excellent bait and tackle.

TIME TO GO...

The day had been excellent and, although Roger and I didn't catch as many as Chris, we were still feeling very content, as we had achieved what we came for. I guess Roger would have liked a ray, but that's just the way it goes. I was just delighted to be out and by the sea doing what I love to do the most, sea angling. Life really doesn't get much better I suppose. There was only one thing left for us to do, and that was to make use of the restaurant and fill up on good food and a cup of tea – a perfect end to a perfect day.

I thoroughly recommend that you get yourselves down to Kent and have a session on one of the most comfortable piers that I have ever fished from. The fishing is great, the surroundings are comfortable and the access is very good indeed.

I would, however, recommend that you call tackle shop Channel Angling in Deal on 01304 373104 in order to obtain some sound advice and the best bait.

Chris proudly displays a typical Deal Pier smoothhound.

The Shore One-Up One-Down Clipped Rig

We reveal some of the best sea angling traces for you to use.

This is a rig that's popular with specialist match anglers and experienced freelance anglers. It's an all-year-round rig, but is especially good in the Christmas and early New Year period when bites can be difficult to come by.

It first appeared around the mid 1970s and became popular on the east coast with dab and whiting anglers, as well as on the south coast and along the west coast of Wales for general species, especially plaice. Such is its effectiveness that it is a rig now used nationwide.

How It Works

The main advantage of this rig is that, having the hooks clipped to the rig body, the whole unit flies cleanly, minimising air drag and adding a few yards of extra distance to the cast. The rig can be used for both long-range and short-range fishing.

More importantly, with the baits being clipped in place in the bait clips, it helps maintain excellent bait presentation after the cast by minimising bait damage during the flight. Also, the rubber rig stop and sequin above each hook keeps the bait tight and compact around the hook and again helps preserve good bait presentation, especially when using smaller, more delicate baits.

By only lightly crimping the crimps holding the bait clips in place, it means that under pressure the crimps will slide, avoiding the hook traces stretching under casting load. If the hook traces stretch and elongate after a few casts, the hooks will not sit tightly in the bait clips and will fall free during the cast.

The reason that this rig is so popular is that it has a wide gap between the hook traces. In deeper water, when the line is at a steeper angle, or when fishing the rig at close range, the top hook bait will be bouncing up and down in the tide and surf surge and will take round fish such as school bass, whiting, coalfish, pout and small codling. The lower hook trace fishes hard on the sea bed, being positioned tight behind the lead weight, and is therefore better placed to take more in the way of dabs and flounders, but in summer will pick out plaice, sole and even turbot.

In shallow water this rig fishes well at close range, too, and you can use a slightly slack line between the rod tip and lead to put both hooks on the sea bed to increase catches of flatfish. But, again, by fishing a tight line it will lift the top bait a little and make it behave differently to attract alternative species.

If you're fishing the surf tables, then the fluorocarbon is important because it's stiffer and will tangle less than standard mono. For normal conditions stick with the 20lb to 25lb ▶

Build Sequence

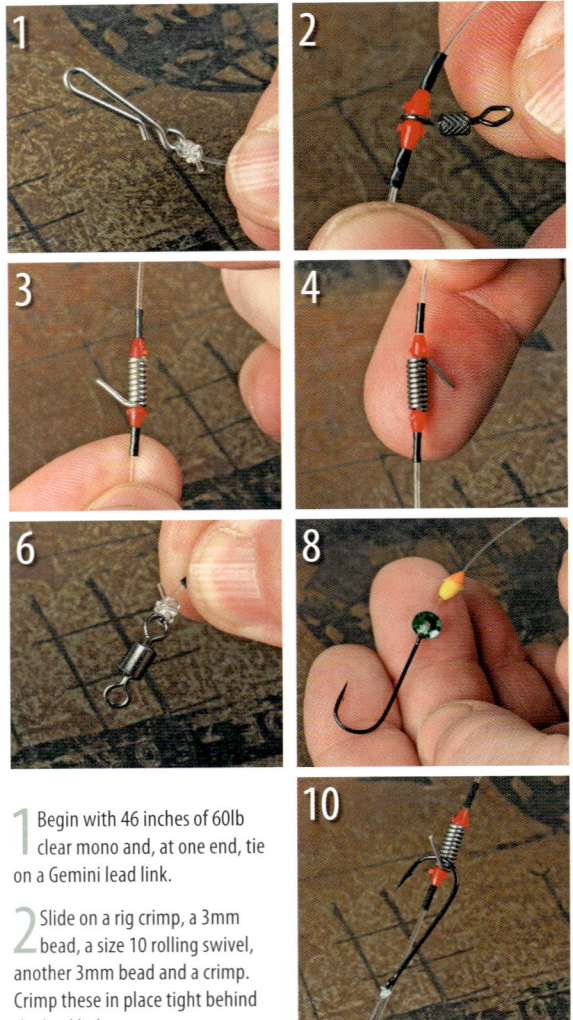

1 Begin with 46 inches of 60lb clear mono and, at one end, tie on a Gemini lead link.

2 Slide on a rig crimp, a 3mm bead, a size 10 rolling swivel, another 3mm bead and a crimp. Crimp these in place tight behind the lead link.

3 Slide on a rig crimp, a 3mm bead, a SALT bait clip (inverted) another bead and a crimp. Leave these loose for now.

4 Slide on a rig crimp, a 3mm bead, a SALT bait clip the right way up, another bead and a crimp. Leave these loose for now.

5 Slide on a rig crimp, a 3mm bead, a size 10 rolling swivel, another 3mm bead and a crimp. Again, leave these loose for now.

6 Finish the main rig by tying on a size 4 rolling swivel.

7 Crimp the top crimp, bead and swivel sequence in place just below the top size 4 swivel.

8 To both hook trace swivels tie on 15 inches of 20lb/25lb fluorocarbon, slide on a rubber rig stop and a sequin, and finish with a size 2 Kamasan B940 Aberdeen hook.

9 Put the bottom hook in the bait clip above it, slide the crimp, beads and bait clip up the trace until the hook trace comes just tight, then crimp the bait clip in place lightly; just tight enough so that you can move it under finger pressure.

10 Put the top hook in the bait clip below, slide the crimps and bait clip down the rig body until the hook trace comes just tight, and again lightly crimp in place just so the clip can move under heavy pressure.

hooklengths, but in calmer seas and daylight, especially when after plaice, then drop down to 12lb or 15lb fluorocarbon.

A good little trick at night is to add a small 3mm luminous bead between the rubber rig stop and sequin above the hook, and charge this in your headlight prior to casting. This can increase your catch rate when targeting dabs, coalfish, rockling, whiting and codling.

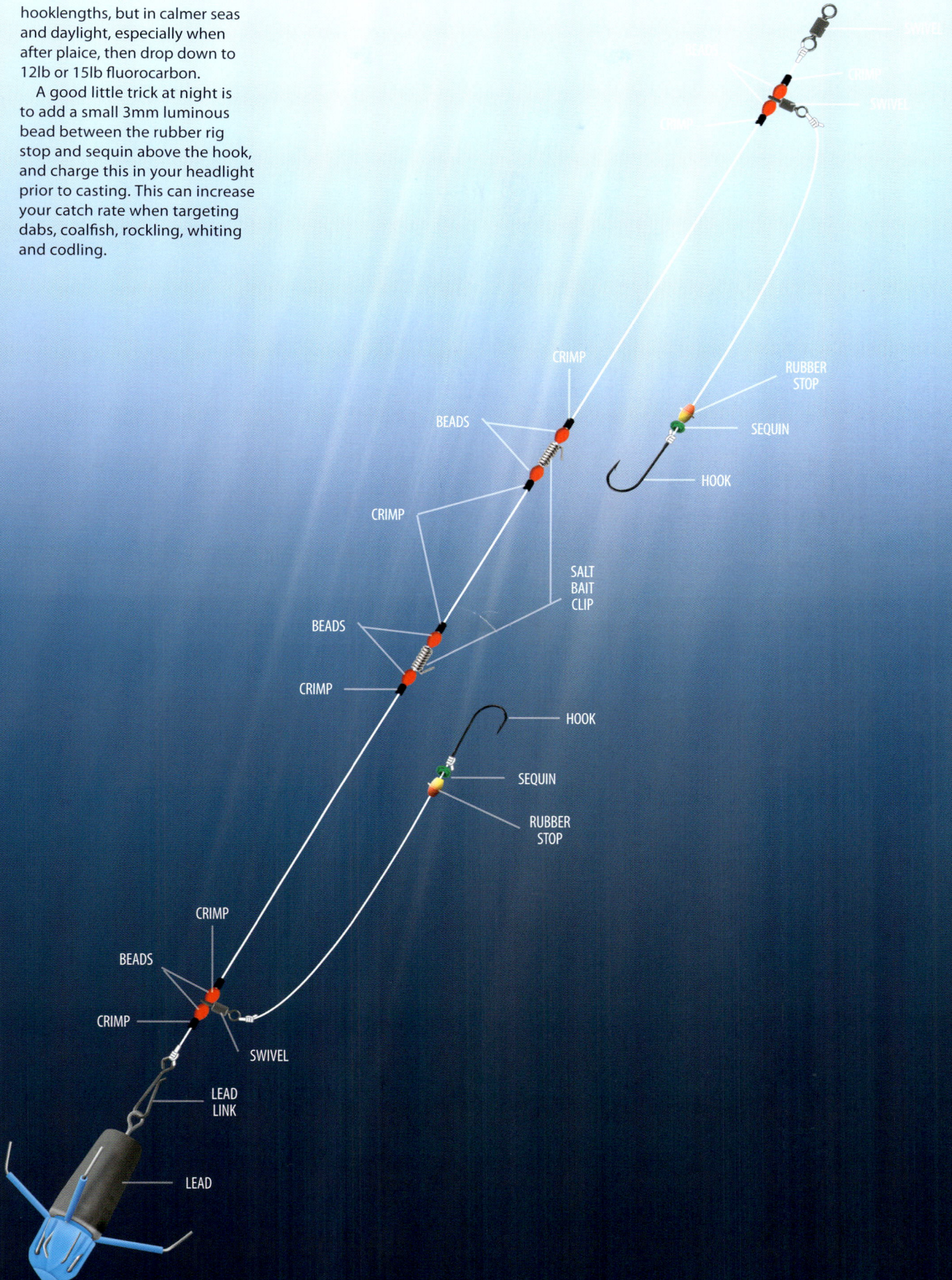

SWIVEL

BEADS

CRIMP

SWIVEL

CRIMP

CRIMP

BEADS

RUBBER STOP

SEQUIN

CRIMP

HOOK

SALT BAIT CLIP

BEADS

HOOK

CRIMP

SEQUIN

RUBBER STOP

CRIMP

BEADS

CRIMP

SWIVEL

LEAD LINK

LEAD

53

Understanding
Wind

David Hall explains how Mother Nature affects our fishing…

Above everything else, wind is the most critical element for anglers and dictates not just how good the fishing may be, but all too often whether we can actually go fishing at all!

Wind is created by the movement of air around the earth – as it shifts from high to low pressure and back again. A westerly wind refers to a wind travelling from a westerly direction and east wind is from the east, and so on.

Wind is officially measured at a specific height above ground: 10 metres or 33 feet. This is because at ground level the wind speed decreases and measurement would lack overall accuracy. In the UK the speed of the wind is measured in knots, or nautical miles per hour, with a knot being 1.15mph, though in most weather forecasts it will be given in true mph.

On a weather page the wind direction and speed are usually shown by an arrow for direction and numbers to indicate the speed. Isobar lines very close together also forecast strong winds. Some weather maps also use the colour red as a warning of gale-force or storm-force winds.

Forecasts will give an average wind speed, but often refer to gusts. Gusts are major variations of wind speed well above that mean average – in fact, they can be 60 per cent higher over land and even 100 per cent higher when channelled through heavily built-up areas inside cities. Wind gusts are higher inland than over the sea or on the windward coast, but mean wind speeds tend to be lower inland. The speeds of gusts are important to boat fishermen and rock anglers. A mean wind speed of 20mph may mean that some areas are fishable, but add gusts to 35mph and the situation can become critical regarding rising sea swells and the possibility of being blown off an exposed rock ledge.

Looking at wind direction, northerly winds tend to be stronger than southerly-based

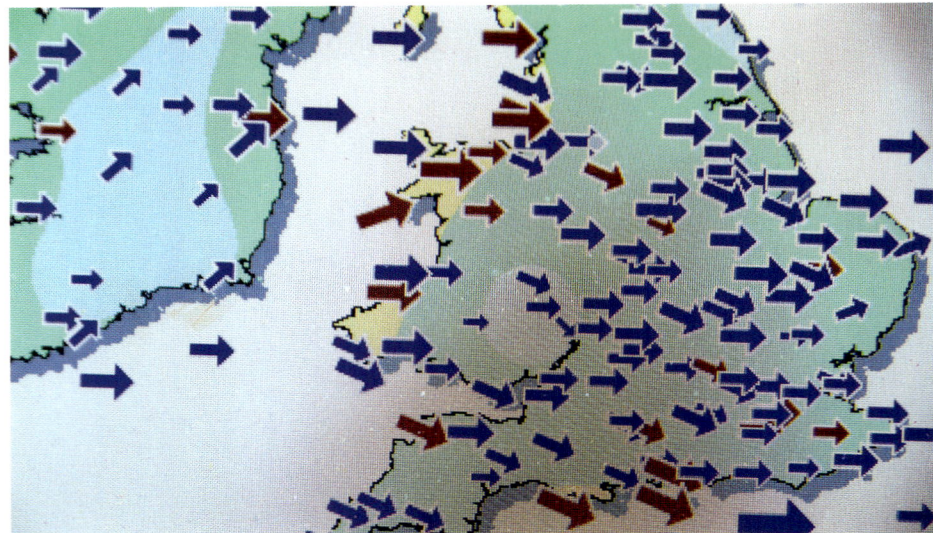

Wind direction is represented by arrows on weather maps, with red indicating gale-force winds.

winds, though there are localised winds that funnel down through estuaries and seaward valleys that cause turbo-like effects and can increase overall wind speed dramatically both onshore and close inshore.

Wind direction also helps us forecast approaching weather. Northerly winds can bring very cold air from the polar region across the UK, especially in winter. As cold polar air moves southwards over an increasingly warmer sea, the air heats up and causes cumulus clouds to develop. These can grow to produce showers, so winds from the northwest, north and northeast tend to bring cold, showery weather over the UK, and possibly snow.

Southerly-based winds bring warm air up from the tropics, but this is cooled as it works north over the gradually cooling sea. This can create ideal conditions for sea fog, or a layer of thin stratus cloud, which can see drizzle, typically on windward coasts and over high ground. Winds from the west or southwest

quarters are more associated with overcast, wet weather.

In summer, winds often come from a southerly or southeasterly direction and bring the UK warm, dry weather, though a southerly wind can also see hot and sticky, thundery weather sometimes.

Cold air from eastern Europe is brought to the UK via an east wind in winter, sometimes straight off the Russian Steppes, and will see very low air temperatures and a severe wind chill. The path and characteristics of this airflow, though, dictate whether it is cloudy with rain, sleet and snow, or fine and sunny. An easterly wind in summer suggests it will be cool on the east coast, but warmer elsewhere, and with clear skies.

Understanding the wind directions and associating these with certain known weather patterns these individual winds bring helps us to use a forecast to greater effect and to choose with more care when, where and even how we should fish.

We

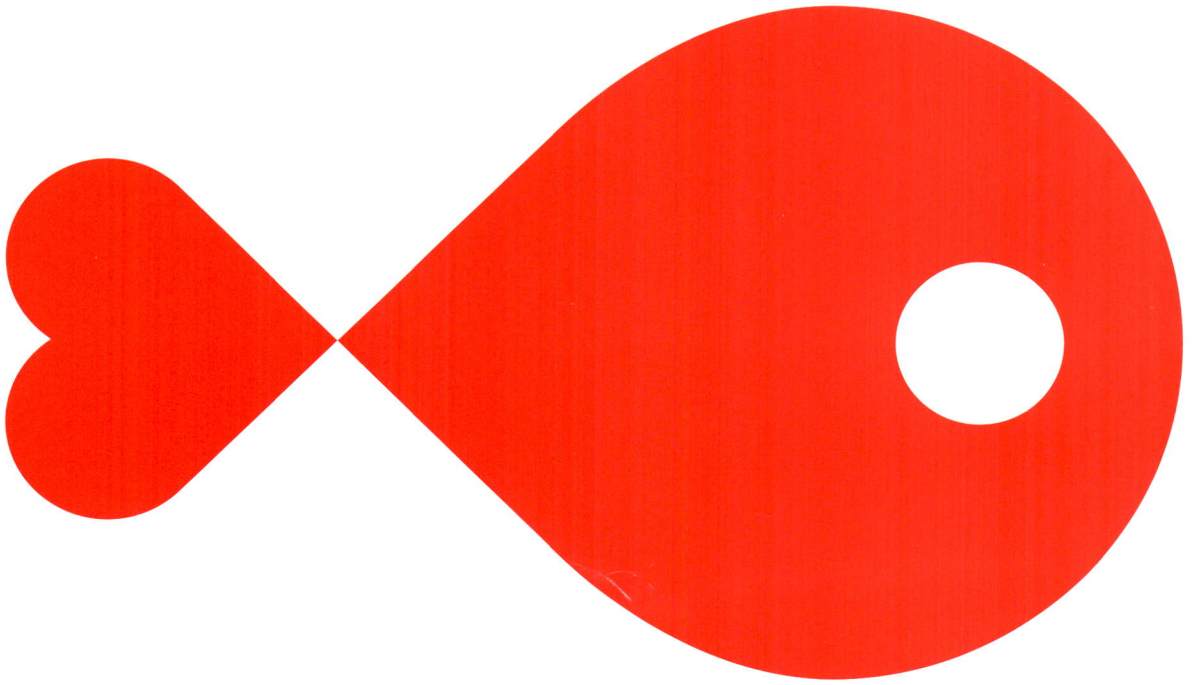

Fishing

—

Because it's a highly effective and proven medium to engage with our young people, especially those in need of support.

For more information about the work we do or our Angling in a Box programme, please contact us:

T +44 (0) 113 815 0087
E hello@ghof.org.uk

www.ghof.org.uk

Registered Charity Number:
England & Wales 1132448, Scotland SC40038.
Company Registration Number: 06800071

GET
HOOKED
ON
FISHING™

Although beaches can appear featureless, there are always areas where fish will congregate.

Surf Beaches

Barney Wright demonstrates how to locate and identify specific fish-holding features on surf beaches.

Watercraft – the art of reading ground features and tide run – is rarely mentioned with regard to shore fishing, yet it's the most important skill a shore angler can learn. For sea fishing beginners, and even some more experienced anglers, fishing unknown areas and identifying exactly where to fish on a surf beach can be a daunting prospect. You're faced with hundreds of yards, maybe even miles, of what looks like featureless sand. This is rarely the case, though, because even if you've fished a mark regularly before, by studying the beach in detail you may be able to identify areas that produce better fishing than you currently enjoy.

This feature will help you identify specific features and little hotspots that anglers often never even realise are there, and the benefit is a huge improvement in your overall catches.

Initial Observation

The first step is to pick out the biggest spring tides during the year. These occur in late March and April, and again in August and September. These tides, especially in high-pressure weather conditions, will travel the maximum distance outwards, exposing ground and features not normally seen on average-sized tides.

It pays to get down on the beach a good hour before low water and just walk the tide line looking back shoreward. Carry a little book and pen to make notes on the things you see.

Even if you have to fish a venue that you haven't seen during the big tides, it's possible on small neap tides when only the minimum of ground is exposed to walk a section of beach and identify numerous areas that will be more productive than just 'chuck and chance it' fishing.

Low water on spring tides will expose most of the features that are usually covered.

SOFT FEATURES

One of the best features to fish on a sand surf beach is a deep gulley. These usually run parallel, or at an angle, along the beach and can be clearly seen. These are caused by a lateral tidal flow. As the tide floods in wave action sees food such as worms, crabs and shellfish washed from the sand and pushed up along the tide line. As the tide floods over the outside bank and into the gulley, that food also gets washed in. As the water deepens and the tide flow starts to flood through the length of the gulley the food is moved along by the tide. These gullies may be only a few feet wide, but they're hotspots for fish congregation.

Fish will access the gulley initially where it meets the sea, and work their way inwards, swimming into the oncoming tide and up the gulley feeding as they go. This is typical of round fish such as bass, whiting and codling. Flatfish can do the same, but often swim up the bank behind the gulley with the tide, then just drop into it and sit on the sand allowing food to be brought to them.

The rising incline of the bank behind the gulley is also a fish-holding feature. Fish such as rays and turbot prefer to feed on the incline sat half buried in the sand while waiting for small prey fish to pass by.

Also note down small sandbanks that are separated by a deeper gulley in the middle. Again the banks offshore will hold fish, but the key area is the narrow gulley in between. These are natural routes for the fish

Scan the beach for gullies that run parallel to the beach because fish will move along these as the tide floods.

to swim through to access the main beach during the flood tide. A bait positioned here will be passed by a higher proportion of fish than one placed in the middle of flat open sand.

Occasionally a small section of beach may have mud mixed in with the sand. This can occur in areas where tide run is minimal and sediment gets deposited. These are good areas for dabs, sole and flounders.

Also watch for slight changes in sand type. Look for sand that is coarser than the surrounding sand. Again, this is caused by tidal action and deposition. These areas will often hold baitfish such as sandeels, and fish like turbot and plaice adopt these as feeding areas.

It's well worth logging down small streams and small rivers that cross the beach. These tend to wash out the finer sand leaving a narrow band of shingle. The ground feature is not so important, but the freshwater is. In the summer and autumn this cools the tide line water down and will induce flounders and bass to work that adjacent stretch of beach hunting for food. These outflows also have smaller flounders resident and big bass will also come in to hunt

these. Often you'll find turbot here too.

At times of flood water after heavy rains, always fish the uptide side of the river or stream. Bass, flounders and even cod will not venture to the downtide side where the acidic water stain is.

HARD FEATURES

Many beaches have areas where the sand butts up to small banks or beds of shingle. The shingle may not hold that much natural food, but what it

Look for a gap in a sand bar. Fish must come through these as the tide rises and you can ambush them here.

Cast into the right areas and you will find fish. Flounders are always present in food-holding areas.

does do is catch and hold food items such as dead fish, washed-out worms and other food stuffs pushed along by the tide flow. The food settles between the shingle and stays there. These catchments are always visited by fish each and every tide.

Also pinpoint patches of bigger boulders and areas of exposed flat rock. This again is a catchment area for waterborne food items washed along by the tide. However, being made from a more static and solid structure, these will also have a permanent population of crabs, seed mussels, periwinkles and other food items. Such areas attract round fish like bass, cod, coalfish, rockling and pouting. If you can stand losing a little kit, then baits in among the snags will fish best. If not, fish as close to the uptide side as you can, allowing the baits' scent to draw the fish out onto clean ground.

Seed and horse mussel beds are always reliable fish-holding features. These beds are typically built over hard rock or a mixture of rock mixed in with fine sand and mud. It's good ground for king rag, crab and inevitably some of the mussels get

Where sand meets rocks and stones are great fish-gathering spots.

The ends of groynes have holes where fish will come each tide to feed.

A mussel bed will attract many species; simply cast onto one to bag up.

broken up too by passing debris, so food is abundant. Bass, codling, coalfish, bigger whiting, but also plaice and big flounders like this type of ground. Cast right on top of it for the best fishing.

Weed beds are always hotspots for fish. These will be clinging to rocky sea beds, though, often covered with sand. Always try to fish on the uptide side of these and let the scent of the bait wash back into the weed bed. If the weed isn't heavy and the tackle is snagging, then cast right into it, as this is where the fish will be working.

Even if a surf beach is devoid of any other feature but has a single big boulder, or several big boulders up above the sand, then these are the markers to fish. All fish will visit these features and, if you look closely, you will see that the tide will have scoured out a hole around the base of the boulder and this again is where food brought on by the tide will collect.

MAN-MADE STRUCTURE AND ROCK OUTCROPS

Some beaches have old concrete sewer pipes – short concrete groynes running out towards the low tide mark. These are natural barriers for food washed along by the tide. The fish, especially flatfish, codling and bass, will always work the bottom edge of the side facing the oncoming tide where the food collects. If you fish the downtide side, move well downtide and fish the ground where the flow of tide coming over the top of the groyne falls back to ground again. This is where the waterborne food will drop and the fish lay in wait. Rays often tend to do this!

The same principle applies to short rocky outcrops. Bass and cod will

work these on the uptide side, but also work around the front of the outcrop lying just inside the tide flow as it passes by. This is a prime spot for bass, which lay in wait for sandeels and other small fish and waterborne food items being washed past. Big flounders can also be taken from these features.

Wooden groynes are often good spots, but are never consistent fish holders along their full length. If you look at the end of groyne at low water you'll more often than not see a scooped-out or dished area at the end. This means accurate casting, but drop a bait in here allowing it to roll into the dish and you will find dabs, turbot, dogfish, flounders, occasional plaice, codling and bass. What you often find is that very few fish, even during a flooding tide, will come inside the groynes. The vast majority of fish will stay out beyond the ends of the groynes and work the open beach. The groynes restrict the tide flow, so there's nothing really to disturb or deposit food.

Old stake-net poles have mussels and barnacles clinging to their sides. Fish will always work around these as they attract smaller prey fish.

WASH-UPS

Another good tactic is to walk the shingle bank of surf beaches along the high tide mark. If you look at the line of weed, wood, sticks, bottles and other assorted junk, you will notice that certain small areas have the majority of the washed-up debris. These indicate areas where the flooding tide current is strongest, and also where food at high water will collect. This is a great place to fish too.

Wash-up zones are where the majority of food will collect.

READING THE SURF

Always study the surf pattern for a few minutes before deciding where to fish if you have no visible feature to work from.

In a heavy surf, look for areas where the surf breaks closer in with calmer water behind. This indicates a deeper hole where food carried by the tide will drop. Fish, such as bass and cod, will pass through here to feed.

In calm seas fish where the surf breaks furthest out and cast as far as you can. This disturbed water will dig out food from the sand, and fish such as bass and flounders will feed even in water just a few inches deep, especially at night or in coloured water.

Areas where surf breaks in an otherwise calmer sea indicates where a rising sandbank lies and, just to the side of these, will be good for bass, plaice, turbot, rays, dabs and whiting. Cast beyond and behind the bank to hit the fish on the incline, or fish the downtide side of the bank for the best effect.

In calm seas rippled water shows the position of weed beds and often

Study where and how the surf breaks to find out where food will be deposited.

Dabs will follow gullies and sand bars in search of food.

rock patches and boulders. But remember that due to the flow of tide, the actual area of surface ripple will be a few yards downtide of the real position of that feature.

HOW TO MARK A HOTSPOT

Having identified a feature, how do you know where it is when the tide floods in? Easy! Stand on the feature and look back to the high tide line. Pick out a marker that you will remember that is dead in line with the feature. Now pace back from the mark to the feature. This will give you an accurate measurement of how far you need to cast with the shoreline marker at your back to reach the feature when the tide floods back in.

Alternatively, some anglers choose to put a small dab of black marker pen onto their reel line having cast a lead to the feature so that they have a visual indication.

Another good tip is to deliberately overcast gutters and gullies, then retrieve the weight and rig until you feel the lead drag up the bank's incline – or, better still, until you feel it drop into the gulley. This is easily felt on the rod tip and cannot be missed.

CONCLUSION

The military says: "Time spent in reconnaissance is never wasted." This is just as true when looking for marks to fish. Take the trouble to explore the venues you usually fish, and especially those you rarely fish, and you will certainly see a dramatic increase in your catch rate.

Also remember that this is an ongoing thing. A single winter storm can take away all the hotspots you previously had, but equally create as many new ones in areas that fished poorly previously.

The Long-And-Low Shore Cod/Bass Rig

TSF reveals some of the best sea angling traces for you to use.

This rig has been around since the mid-1970s and has become one of the most consistent rigs used by anglers targeting a wide variety of fish, including cod, bass, huss and rays.

This particular rig uses minimal components – making it streamlined for casting, less likely to snag, plus it's inexpensive to replace if you lose it when fishing over mixed rough ground, or when bringing fish back over potential snags. With the cod season just about to get under way in many areas, you shouldn't be without this.

How It Works

The advantage of this rig is that after casting, the bait falls free of the rig clip, the hooklength comes free from the bait clip, and it all flows out in the tide. Because the hooklength is secured tight behind the bottom rig clip, this means the bait is fishing hard on the sea bed but has the freedom to move in the tide giving natural presentation. This is especially effective when fishing deep water close in, but also at long range in rough seas when you need to know that the bait is tight on the sea bed where the fish are hunting.

Another advantage is that as a fish takes the bait and turns away into the tide, it comes up hard against the grip-wire lead and will self-hook, mostly avoiding deep hooking.

The other major advantage is that when the fish is hooked and being fought, the lead weight is up above the fish and will hopefully miss the worst of any snags as the fish is retrieved.

The loop for holding hooks at the end of the hooklength is also critical.

Using this means that there are two lengths of line hidden inside the bait, increasing the strength and reducing the chances of a fish being lost due to abrasion. The top hook is also stronger secured on the double line than it is using a conventional 'wrap the hooklength around the hook shank' system, which most anglers use for positioning the top hook of a Pennel rig.

Also, the top hook, being held only by the eye and trapped between the bead and the bottom granny knot, can be fully turned upside down then passed through the middle of a big worm bait and out again to provide perfect presentation. The bead just acts as a stop to avoid the bait and the top hook pushing backwards up the hooklength through casting pressure.

This rig is also excellent for big autumn bass when fishing whole squid baits into the surf, or when casting from steep beaches and man-made structures into deep water.

Build Sequence

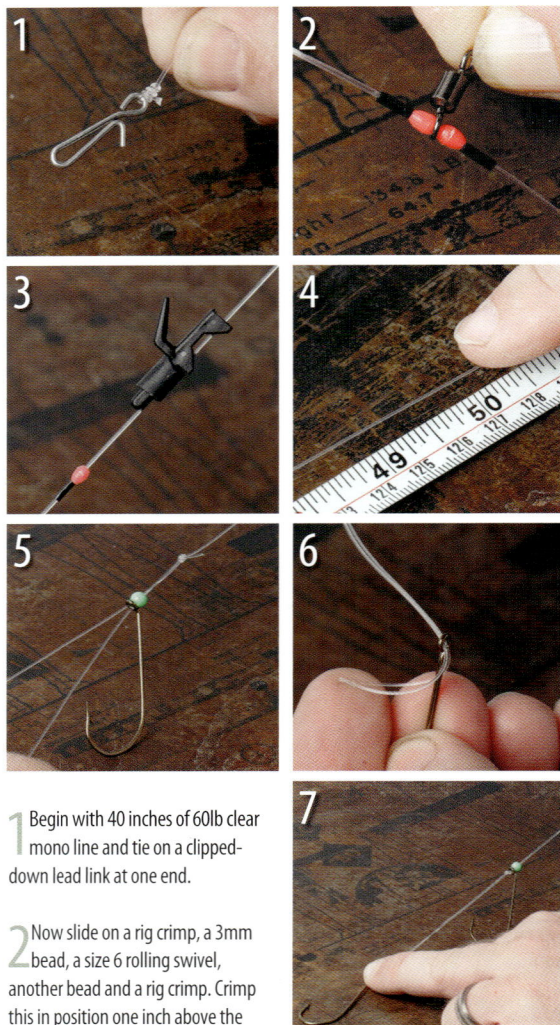

1 Begin with 40 inches of 60lb clear mono line and tie on a clipped-down lead link at one end.

2 Now slide on a rig crimp, a 3mm bead, a size 6 rolling swivel, another bead and a rig crimp. Crimp this in position one inch above the lead link.

3 Slide on a rig crimp, a 3mm bead and an inverted Breakaway bait clip – leave these loose for now and, to the free end of the mono, tie on a quality size 4 rolling swivel to complete the rig's body.

4 The hooklength needs to be about 50 inches of 30lb clear mono or fluorocarbon. Use 40lb if you're fishing over snags.

5 On the free end of the hooklength form a loop about six inches long, depending on the intended bait size, and tie in an overhand granny knot. Slide on a size 5mm bead, then a size 4/0 Mustad 79510 Viking hook by passing the end of the loop through the eye of the hook.

6 Tie in another granny knot two inches below the hook and bead. Take a Mustad Viking 79515 hook and thread the end of the loop through the eye, then pass the hook through the loop and pull tight to the eye.

7 Put the hook trace in the inverted bait clip and the bottom hook in the rig clip. Slide the bait clip up or down until the hooklength comes just tight. Crimp the bait clip in place leaving just half an inch below the clip for this to slide in.

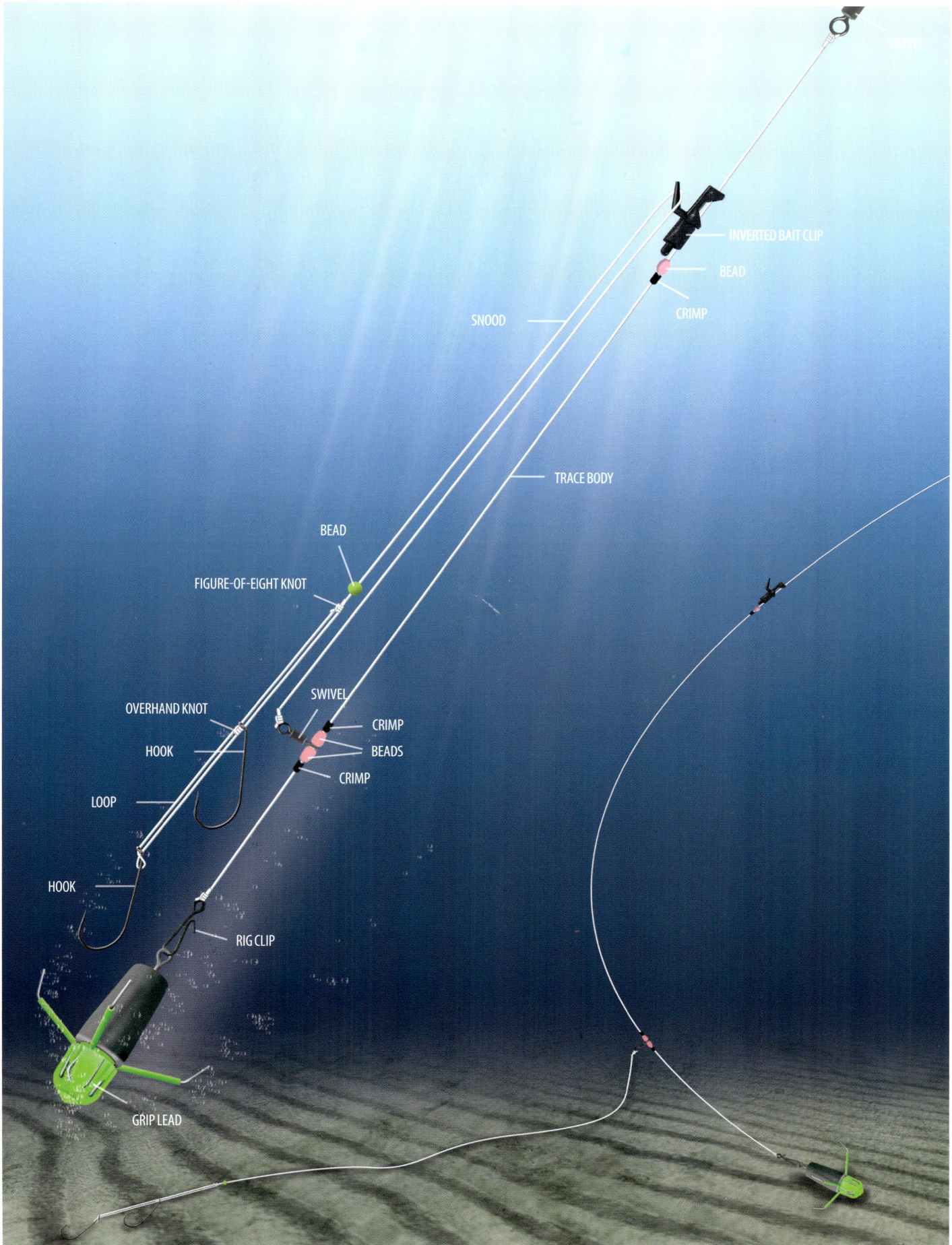

SWIVEL

INVERTED BAIT CLIP

BEAD

CRIMP

SNOOD

TRACE BODY

BEAD

FIGURE-OF-EIGHT KNOT

SWIVEL

OVERHAND KNOT

CRIMP

HOOK

BEADS

CRIMP

LOOP

HOOK

RIG CLIP

GRIP LEAD

The Figure-Of-Eight Loop Knot

Learn how tie a super-strong knot.

We show you possibly the strongest knot available to attach you leader line to – even the editor was taken by surprise! It's easy to tie and also has more than one application, as it can also be used to build a simple, but strong, rig.

*Top*tips

Always ensure that you pull any knot in a straight line. The tyer's hand is holding the hooklength that leaves two snoods. Never use the top snood because this will be very weak. Any pressure will not be exerted through the knot but against it. You may think that this is best to avoid the hooklength twisting around the main line. Well it does not work like that and when we talk about line we will explain why.
Simply tie your lower dropper to a very good swivel and attach your weights.

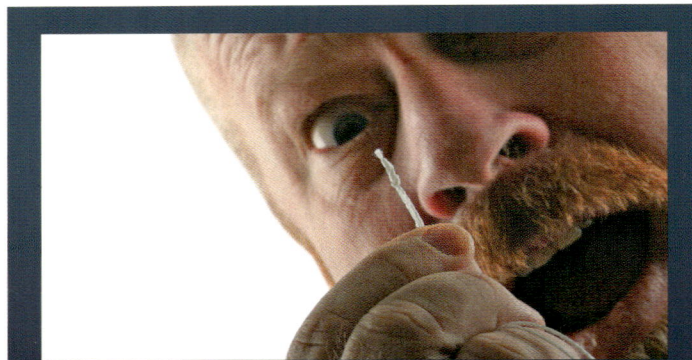

Think you know it all?

Barney Wright, the editor, needed some convincing that the figure-of-eight knot was stronger than a spider hitch.

We only need to master a few knots to cover all of our fishing situations and a figure-of-eight is certainly one of them. Some 30 years ago the spider hitch was a popular knot for making a quick double line. However, after top angler Roy Marlow, who requires 'extreme' knots for 'extreme' fishing, lost a striped marlin due to the line breaking easily at this knot, he soon changed his mind.

Years later and even more tests have proved that the spider hitch is insufficient for extreme fishing, so why not use it as part of your leader knot as well?

On test, Barney's spider hitch knot broke before his figure-of-eight knot did; his face, above, says it all!

How To Tie The Figure-Of-Eight Knot

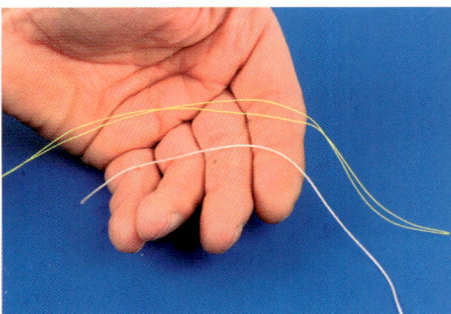

Lay your leader material alongside the double line.

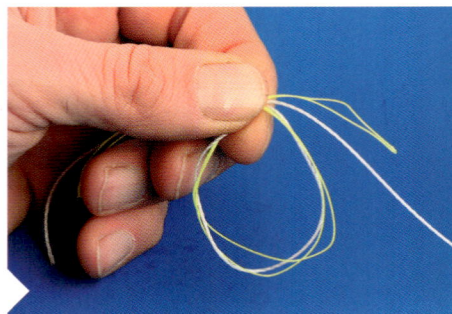

Form a loop, pinching the coils.

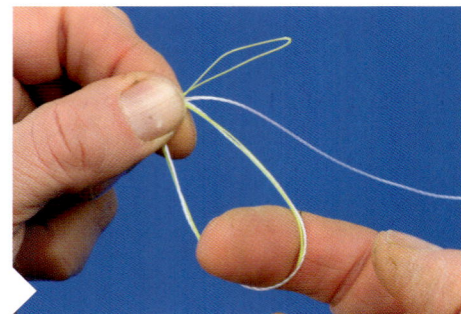

Insert your right-hand index finger through the loop from behind…

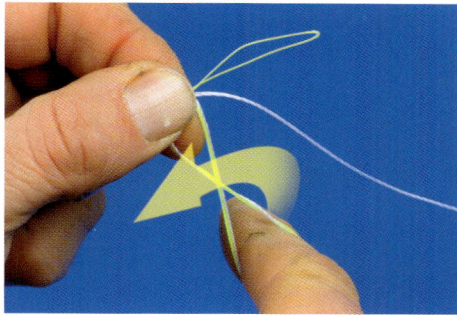
... twist once...

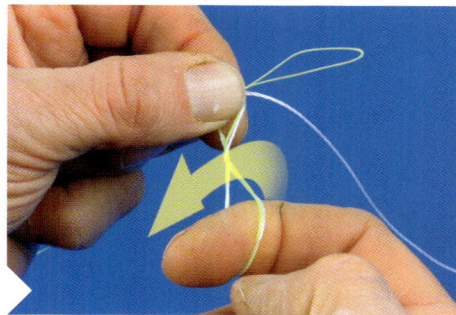
... twist twice.

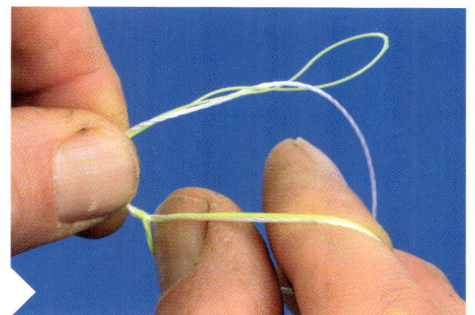
Push your thumb and forefinger through the big loop.

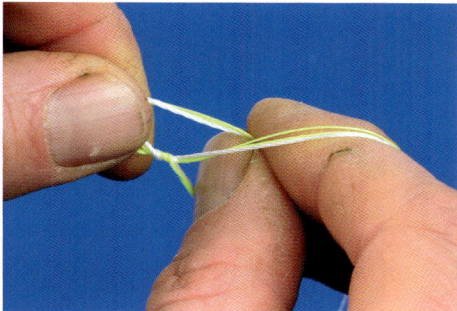
Grip the loop and the leader material.

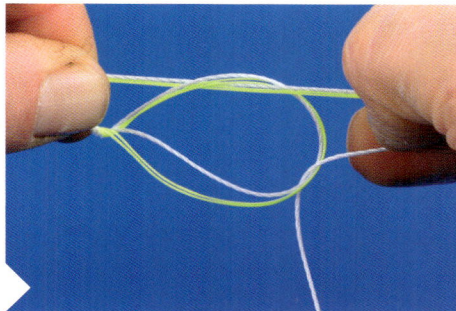
Pull it all through, including your entire leader.

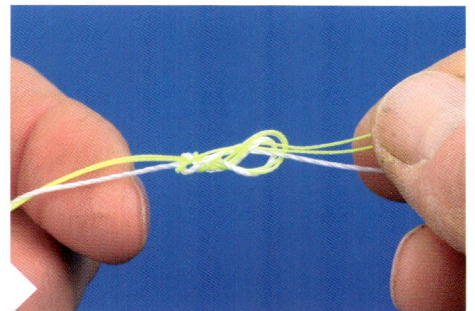
Slowly pull all of the ends so that they close evenly, making sure that you have the magic eight shapes.

Lubricate and pull tight, holding the pressure on for several seconds to allow the coils to fully settle.

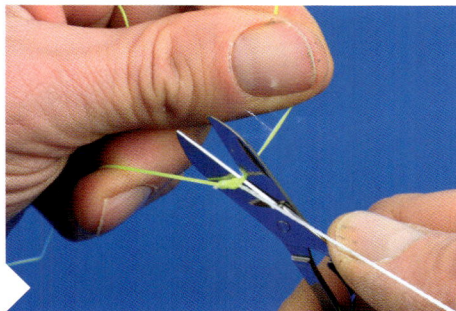
Snip off as close as you wish.

NOW THAT'S SIMPLE, but just think what you have achieved. Your weakest knot is the first figure-of-eight loop but, next to a Bimini, this is the strongest knot that we know for forming a double line. There is no way that if you pull for a break that it will break at this knot. You have a small, compact knot that will offer minimum resistance through the guides and is less likely to pick up on your fixed-spool reel if you're using a long leader. Now that you've mastered this knot, you can adapt it for several rigs very quickly. This shows a very simple paternoster rig that is very popular and catches loads of fish. Again the figure-of-eight knot has been used to form this leader. If you want the entire leader to be the same material as your main line, just form a big loop and snip according to the lengths that you want. Or, simply lay your leader material alongside and tie it in.

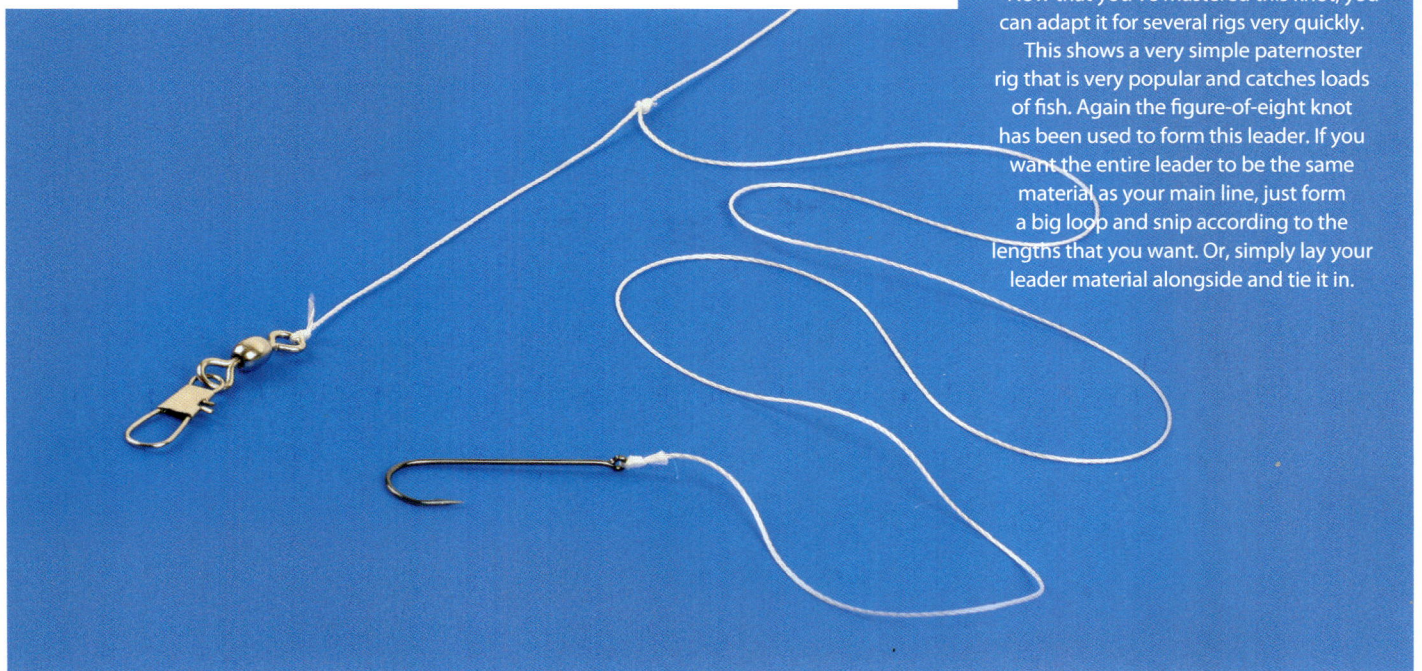

How To Use
Mackerel

Catch, prepare and store this juicy bait for the hook.

Mackerel are easy to find. You can catch your own, buy them fresh from a fishmonger or supermarket, or get them blast frozen from your local tackle shop.

When the mackerel are 'in' during the summer months, it's easy to bag up with dozens of them, so only take what you need for food or bait.

You will catch your share of mackerel on feathers, spinners and floats, and while casting feathers will catch more, spinning and float fishing with light tackle is more fun.

Being a common, natural food, mackerel can be fished as bait in just about every sea – whether you're using the whole fish or just a tiny strip. A strip of mackerel can be used on its own or to tip off other baits to add flavour and colour for bottom rigs and float fishing.

They can be cut into chunks for rays and bass, fillets for bass, turbot and brill, or the backbone can be removed to make a flapper for congers, bass and tope.

KEEPING THEM FRESH
If you're able to catch your own mackerel and want to keep some as bait for another day, you'll need to get them into a cool box packed with ice to keep them as fresh as possible. If you want to keep a lot of mackerel for bait, it pays to fillet them as soon as they're caught. Mackerel are oily fish and their flesh will start to break down as soon as they're dead, so put them in a zip-lock freezer bag and store in the ice; this way you can store fresh bait ready for future trips. Make sure you put them straight into the freezer as soon as you get home, though.

Mackerel are superb bait for most sea fish, and they're good to eat.

How To Bait Up With Mackerel...

When the mackerel are 'in', even the youngsters can bag up as the fish come in close to the beach.

Small strips of mackerel are great for tempting black bream, gurnards, garfish and mackerel.

When taking a fillet off, always cut away from your fingers.

A fillet mounted like this is perfect for brill, turbot, bass and rays.

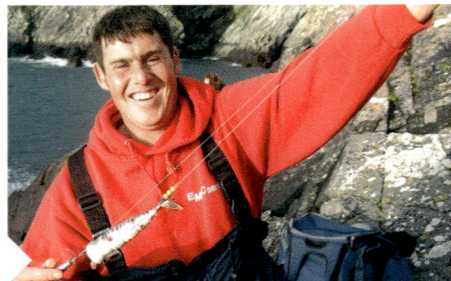

A whole mackerel can be mounted on a Pennel rig and cast from the shore for congers and bull huss.

A mackerel flapper is one of the top baits for congers, tope and sharks.

Leka The Jewel In The Crown

Barney Wright ventured to an island just off the coast of mid-Norway and encountered a whole load of new and exciting fishing experiences…

Norway is an angling paradise, providing some of Europe's finest sea fishing, so it's little wonder that each year fishermen from far and wide home in on the country to capitalise on the extraordinary sport being offered in these well-managed waters.

While other shorelines are being plundered and overfished, the Norwegians ensure their stocks remain high by enforcing sensible commercial rules. As a result, it has become a true angling El Dorado.

And things are about to get even better for visiting anglers because a fishing camp is to be opened shortly on the island of Leka, in mid-Norway. Called Leka Brygge, it was started in 1998 then encountered a series of hold-ups and delays, but thanks to plenty of perseverance the place is now ready to open its doors to anglers.

I recently became one of the first to experience this new camp and sample the fishing on offer. My trip was with Norwegian holiday

company Din Tur, and my guide was Ian Peacock, the managing director of its UK base, along with top northeast angler Gary Pye. Both are excellent anglers and often travel together to seek out new venues for UK fishermen to visit – both from the boat and shore.

This was my sixth visit to Norway, and each time I feel privileged in the knowledge that I am about to experience a new area providing largely untapped fishing. Leka was no different and, as we made our

This pollack wolfed down the Isome worm fished on a 3g jighead.

Barney Wright is delighted with this cracking 7lb pollack that fell for LRF tactics.

way there on the final internal flight, I gazed out of the plane's window and was awestruck by some of the glorious sights as we followed the coastline. But deep down I was really imagining all the magnificent fish we'd flown over – most of which would have never encountered a baited hook!

NO MESSING

The first thing we did after offloading our luggage into the accommodation was to grab some tackle and jump into one of the tinny, self-hire boats that are freely available for anglers to use.

These vessels comfortably fish four so it was bliss for the three of us. We steamed out just a few hundred yards and into a channel in front of the camp where we sent down some lures and were instantly into fish – if only all fishing was as easy as this.

We were only in 20 metres of water, but the wind was pushing us hard making lure presentation tricky – nevertheless, the fish were obliging and we had a fair haul of cod, pollack and a mountain of mackerel, but as we drifted along I couldn't help but notice an area by a bridge that looked perfect for a spot of light rock fishing (LRF). This is something that I've been itching to do in Norway, as I've enjoyed fabulous success with fishing ultra-light tackle in the UK. I have learnt that fish of any size will hit even very small baits, as the England Boat squad constantly prove. Using the tactic in Norway could be a real eye-opener.

GOING LIGHTLY IN LEKA...

A few casts off a ledge with a 3oz jighead and an artificial Marukyu Isome worm into about 20 metres of water resulted in loads of small coalfish to begin with – then all hell broke loose when a decent-sized pollack took a fancy to the 'lure'. Ian had already bagged a nice specimen on a Sidewinder using standard shore spinning gear, and, while it gave him a wonderful scrap, the reality was that the fish never stood a chance on that tackle. So you can imagine how I felt with a 7lb pollack thrashing away at the end of my gossamer-like gear – it was BRILLIANT!

A fish that could have easy been headskulled in with a few cranks of a heavy reel took me several minutes on the light tackle. It was comparable to battling a 40lb cod on standard boat gear, and to enjoy a 'lesser-sized' fish in Norway to such an extent opened up a

whole new world for me, and the sport this country already offers was taken to a totally new level. Even the mackerel felt like hard-fighting tuna as they pounced on my offerings.

The sport was awesome and I was reluctant to stop fishing but there was a whole island to explore and we needed to plan the following day's trip before snatching a few hours' sleep. But I also made a vow to myself – the LRF gear

would be constantly with me wherever we ventured.

WEATHER RULES

As with every fishing trip, the weather plays a big part, but with Leka being an island it's always possible to find some areas where conditions are spot on. So hopes were high when we decided to

A cracking 15lb cod that took a coalfish hooked on a Gummimakk.

You can see that this cod went for a coalfish that was already hooked on a lure.

head north the following day for a crack at the halibut grounds, but those lovely great flatties had gone AWOL and we simply had to make do with a boatful of cod up to 8lb!

TIME FOR A COMMERCIAL…
Although we drew a halibut blank, a local boat skipper offered to take us for a trip to his secret hunting grounds on his commercial boat, which found us the following day weaving in and out of small islands and through gaps between land that, in truth, made the three of us nervous, before reaching the open ocean where there was nothing but water between us and Greenland!

We asked if we could go for some big cod, but a language barrier ended up with us being taken to some coalfish grounds instead – I really must learn Norwegian!

WHEN IN ROME
Expecting some kind of secret rig to be explained to us, the skipper deployed an ultra-basic setup of a couple of Gummimakks behind a monstrous pirk. I'm not a big fan of thumping a massive lump of metal up and down, so left that to Gary and Ian to crack while I rigged up something a little more sensitive. I began by fishing a shad on a running leger before switching to a jumper rig – basically a French boom that allows you to fish above the sea bed and enables more action to be put into artificial lures.

Gary and Ian were hitting big coalies every drop on the pirks, whereas I was only bringing up small ones – and not very many at that! The water was 150 metres deep and having to reel all that line in for a small fish was not really worth the effort so, biting the bullet, I switched to the brutal stuff and was quickly into big coalies.

THANK COD!
As I was working away with the coalies, Gary was hit by something that offered a far more heavy, head-thumping fight, which turned out to be a pristine 25lb cod. The fish was to be the best specimen of the trip, although I would not have swapped the sport I enjoyed from the pollack on the lighter gear for it. For me, those fish were a better result pro rata.

GOLDFISH
Our next mission was to go right around the island, stopping off at as many spots as possible – mainly reefs and drop-offs – and each fresh location resulted in cod, coalies and torsk, along with the occasional redfish and pollack.

At one spot on the south side of the island we noticed the incredible red rock in the mountains, and it was here that we caught cod that were heavily speckled with deep, dark markings while their golden colouring resembled more like that of a goldfish – truly

incredible. The sea bed and food in the area must be extremely varied to account for this and the experience was yet another first.

CATCH MY DRIFT
We finished the day with several long drifts on the north side of the island in just 15 metres of water, where I set a rod to drift bait just off the sea bed for a cod or halibut and secured it to the boat before my LRF gear was once more deployed. I was instantly into some fantastic sport with mackerel – they really are game fish and it's a shame they don't grow to double figures. I also hooked into something that offered a dogged battle slightly different from that of a mackerel, which turned out to be a surprise – my first-ever Norwegian garfish.

It looked around the 2lb mark but it dropped off because some hungry seagulls tried to attack it as I reeled

Leka Rocks!
The geology of Leka appears to be different from the rest of Norway as its rock type is the youngest, at a mere 10,000 years old. On the west of the island the red coloration of the mountains is most noticeable, and this is known locally as the 'ophiolite complex'. Leka is one of only four places in the world where this occurs, the others being Oman, Cyprus and California – which is something of a mystery.

It's a cracker – a cod that's coloured like a goldfish, and a first for Barney!

we finally had a go with the beachcasters!

We tackled several marks, mostly easy access such as piers or jetties, but also trekked to a couple of hard-to-access marks that the more hardy UK visitor may prefer. Every spot produced cod and coalfish, but we only spent an hour or less at each mark simply to see if they were viable spots. There were snags at all the venues, but the rewards cancel out the worries of any gear loss.

We finished the day at the harbour where we had boarded the commercial boat, and found one of our favourite marks.

Ian hauled out cod and pollack from the inside of the harbour, where the water was so clear that you could see the fish take, while Gary and I stuck to the outside and a cast of only 50 metres saw us in the same depth of water! Needless to say we had plenty of cod to finish this trip – it was literally a fish a chuck.

A BIT OF PERSPECTIVE
Norway has become famous for giving anglers the chance of hooking into jumbo cod of 40lb plus, but putting all of the emphasis on these massive fish is, in my opinion, a little sad. You have to remember that boating a 40lb cod in Norway is akin to catching a 10lb or 15lb equivalent in the UK, so while it is an achievement it's not that extra special. And if you want a personal-best cod from the shore it's there for the taking. I have never caught a double-figure shore cod in the UK but I have reeled in plenty to 15lb in Norway, although a 20lb-plus fish still eludes me.

Catching big fish is obviously a thrill but even if you only catch run-of-the-mill pollack and cod, the chances are that it will all add up to the best fishing you'll ever experience – the sort of sport you can only dream about in the UK.

Every time I travel to Norway I leave feeling that I've found my new favourite spot, but the reality is that the whole of Norway is my favourite place to be.

it towards the boat and in my bid to keep it away from the scavengers the hook-hold worked loose as I bullied it.

We boated endless mackerel, cod and coalies in this shallow water – so many that our arms were aching.

TALKING POLLACKS
Our penultimate day saw us drift the same area and I hooked into another big fish on the LRF gear. Hoping I could possibly create a Norwegian cod LRF record I played the fish carefully but it turned out to be a pollack,

almost identical to the one I had from the shore using the same gear! The fight was great, but I must be honest and admit that the shore fish gave me more pleasure – there's something special about a good fish caught from the shore and it somehow seems more of a challenge than from a boat.

The wind suddenly picked up to serious speeds and ominous-looking dark clouds began to appear on the horizon. It was a case of full steam ahead for the 30-minute journey back to base and we made it just before

a wall of rainwater driven by strong winds pounded the area.

A SHORE THING
Having spent much of our time on the boat, flitting from mark to mark around the island, we felt that we should enjoy at least one full day dedicated to the shore. Every few hundred metres we travelled on the boat, we would look for some shore marks we'd like to try but, as you can imagine, it's hard to change tactics when things are going well, so it wasn't until the last day that

The Alderney Rig

We reveal some of the best sea angling traces for you to use.

The Alderney rig has been around for some 25 years or so, but its history is vague. It is highly likely, though, that, due to its name, it was invented by anglers fishing live sandeels and joey mackerel over the prolific sandbanks off Alderney and the Channel Islands for bass, turbot and rays.

As ever there are a few slight variations to the original rig, which basically used a swivel trapped between two beads sliding freely on a section of clear 40lb mono about five feet long. The rig described below is a personal variation that has worked not just in the Channel Islands for the TSF team, but also off the west coast of Wales and the west coast of Ireland.

How It Works

This rig works best in a tidal run when drift fishing over sandbanks, but will also produce when drift fishing over shallow wrecks and even reefs.

With the hook-trace swivel free to slide up and down on the rig body, it allows bigger sandeels, such as launce, to swim more freely in the water column and be presented more naturally.

The neoprene stop knot allows the angler to adjust the height that the sandeel or bait swims at. As you drift, the water pressure slides the swivel and bait down towards the lead weight. Without the neoprene stop knot the bait would end up fishing tight on the sea bed, which is fine if you're after turbot, brill and rays sitting on a sandy incline hard on the sea bed.

However, it's no good when fishing for bass that are free-swimming predators – often near the sea bed or just up off the bottom – looking upwards and using the light of the surface water to silhouette their prey against. You now have the option of ▶

Build Sequence

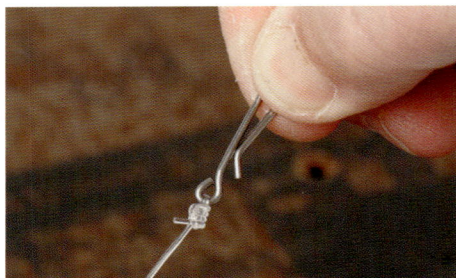

Take a 7ft 6in length of 60lb clear mono line. At one end tie on a Gemini lead link.

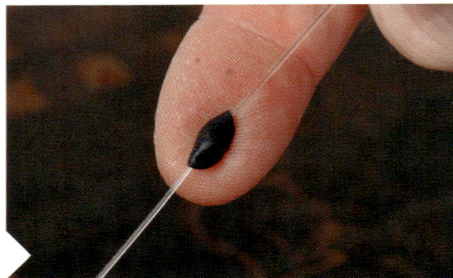

Cut a ½in length of neoprene tubing. Slide this onto the line, then double the line back through the original end and pull tight to form a big sliding stop knot.

Now slide on a 5mm bead, a size 4 rolling swivel and another bead.

To the remaining free end tie on a size 4 rolling swivel to complete the rig body.

The hook trace needs to be 18lb to 25lb fluorocarbon or mono when targeting bass, but if you're after rays, heavier 30lb fluorocarbon or mono is the wiser choice. The hook trace should be seven feet in length or longer.

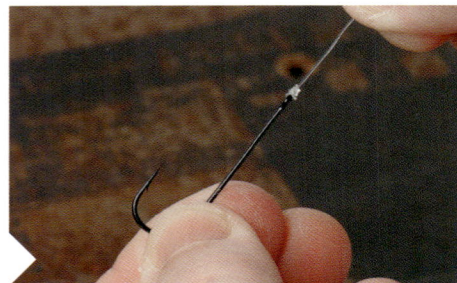

Hook choice depends on the type and size of bait. For average-size sandeels, a size 1 or 1/0 Kamasan B940 Aberdeen is about right. When fishing small joey mackerel, go up to a size 3/0 Mustad Viking 79515 or a Sakuma equivalent.

sliding the stop knot up a few feet away from the lead link to lift the sandeel well up off the sea bed, and allow the predators below a better view of their target.

Lifting the bait up off the sea bed also works better when using small joey mackerel for bass fishing. This works well over sandbanks, but also when working tight over shallow wrecks and when looking to drop baits over the edge of reefs, which is highly effective due to its natural presentation.

This rig does need some tidal flow, though, to aid good presentation by keeping the hook trace at a right angle to the rig body. You also need to let the rig down through the water column slow and steady to prevent tangles. Making the hook trace from fluorocarbon will also help reduce tangles, as it's slightly stiffer than comparable mono, therefore, giving better presentation. In addition, fluorocarbon will help increase the number of bites you get in clear water, as it's less easy for the fish to see than plain mono. This is borne out in experienced anglers' catches, who typically won't use mono for any form of hook trace in daylight.

The reason this variation is made with a heavy 60lb rig body is that the rig often surprises and will hook big blonde rays, pollack and even cod. The full weight of the fish will be fought

with the swivel eye pressurising the rig-body line directly. Having the 60lb gives good strength and maximum reliability when playing fish of this size.

Another advantage of the rig is that it uses minimal rig components. Bass in clear shallow water can be spooky and are often put off by big sliding booms passing by, even when fishing long 15ft traces on flying-collar rigs. This rig minimises its visual structure as it passes by and, more often than not, it will produce a bigger catch ratio for you.

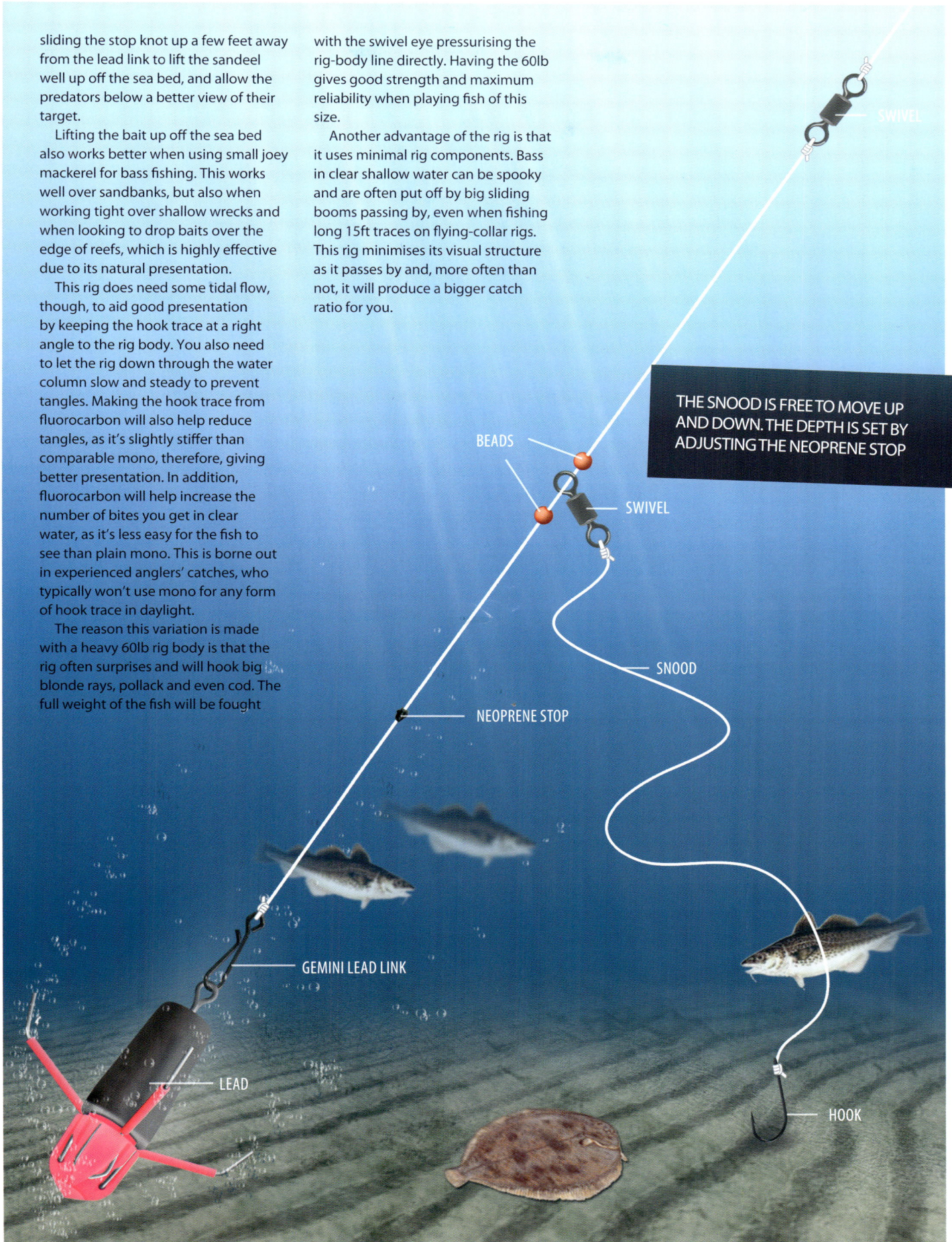

SWIVEL

THE SNOOD IS FREE TO MOVE UP AND DOWN. THE DEPTH IS SET BY ADJUSTING THE NEOPRENE STOP

BEADS

SWIVEL

SNOOD

NEOPRENE STOP

GEMINI LEAD LINK

LEAD

HOOK

Understanding
Wind & Tides

TSF explains how Mother Nature affects our fishing…

A strong wind pushing out a big ebb tide will expose more sea bed.

Understanding how the direction of the wind affects the tide and sea conditions is vital to successful fishing and bait collecting.

Your tide table will indicate the predicted time of low water and the mean low-water height it should achieve. However, if the wind is coming off the land and blowing out to sea, this will produce an actual low-tide time slightly later than is forecast, because the water will be held back briefly by the offshore wind pushing against it.

More importantly, a strong offshore wind will push the tide substantially further out than predicted. This is especially useful for bait collectors to know during the biggest spring tides, as it uncovers ground that doesn't normally dry out and exposes worm or razorfish beds, which will have had little if any digging pressure because they normally remain covered by water.

Equally, as the tide floods and reaches high water, a strong offshore wind will hold the sea back a little, producing a high-water height a little less than predicted. The stronger the wind, the greater the effect on the tidal height – with the height of the tide peaking slightly earlier than predicted too.

It works the opposite way with an onshore wind and flooding tide. This results in the water not receding as far back as predicted over low water, plus the tide will turn and flood back inwards slightly earlier than predicted too. With a strong onshore wind coming off the sea and a big spring tide, the high tide will be higher than predicted as it's pushed in further with the wind behind it, and turn fractionally later than the given high-tide time too as it's held back for longer.

A change in wind speed and direction will often be triggered by low-water and high-water slack, the period when the tide is in transition between changing from flood to ebb and vice versa. This will usually be a strengthening wind appearing with the change to a flooding tide, and often a decreasing wind as the tide ebbs.

These slack-water periods can also trigger a change in wind direction with an ebbing tide, which often sees the wind swing in a clockwise rotation and decrease, and a change to a flood tide sees the wind turn anti-clockwise and increase in speed. These tend to be localised changes and are not noted nationally.

A change of tide and wind direction can also see rain or clearer weather move in with a newly flooding tide, but ease away to showers or nothing on the ebb.

When boat fishing on the drift, then a wind blowing in the same direction as the tide will increase the drift speed significantly, making it almost impossible to fish, or at least require the use of much heavier leads to maintain contact with the sea bed.

In areas where the tide run is fast or very fast, then the ideal wind is one that is blowing in the opposite direction to the run of tide. This has the effect of holding a boat back and slowing the drift speed down. This is often the ideal wind when shark fishing because it allows the boat to drift slowly but the fast tide will carry any rubby-dubby scent trail far away.

By being aware of these changes in the tide and the way it is affected by the wind, it makes us more aware of the possible conditions and puts us in a more favourable position to anticipate how these conditions will affect the fish that we target.

Find your own
Peeler Crabs

How to collect and prepare peelers for the hook.

Peelers can be found under weed-covered rocks.

As crabs get bigger they have to grow a new skin, shedding their old hard shell. Once the shell is discarded they become vulnerable to attack from other crabs and fish, so hide away under rocks and seaweed until their new skin hardens. The crabs start peeling in the spring, usually around April or May, when the water temperature reaches about 10 degrees, and may peel two to three times during the spring and summer months until the temperature drops in the autumn.

WHERE

Peeling shore crabs can be found at low tide under weed-covered boulders, groynes and pier piles. It can be difficult to tell a peeler from a hard crab; sometimes you can tell just by looking at it as the shell can be dull and may be starting to crack and lift. A sure method is to remove the last segment of the rear leg by gently twisting and pulling it off. If it's a peeler the hard shell will be empty and you'll see the new fleshy segment exposed.

Once you've collected a few peelers, keep them cool in a bucket covered in wet seaweed then transfer them to your bait fridge. You can store them in cat-litter trays covered in seaweed and they'll keep for several days but you must keep them cool and check them daily – removing any dead crabs immediately.

PREPARATION

To prepare them for bait you must remove all the hard shell, removing the legs first then the belly and back shell. They can be used whole for cod, bass and smoothhound, or cut into pieces for small species or to tip off worm baits. Once you have the crab on the hook you'll need to secure it in place with fine bait elastic, as the fish will soon rip off the soft flesh.

How To Bait Up With Peeler Crab...

If the shell is starting to lift, it's a peeler!

Another way to check is to remove the end section of the back leg.

Take off all the legs and claws, then all of the hard shell.

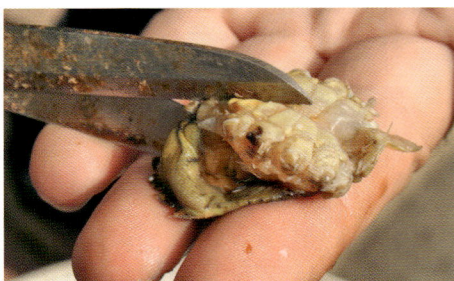

Once you've got rid of all the hard shell, cut the crab in half...

... and stitch the hook through the soft flesh as many times as you can.

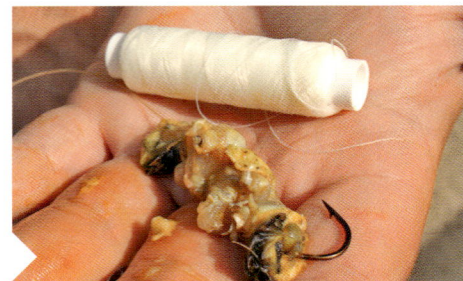

Finally, secure the crab with bait elastic.

The Rapala Knot

We show you the best way to attach your lures to your line so that your artificial baits are allowed to work most effectively.

To allow a lure to move as 'naturally' as possible, it makes sense to have it attached to your line via a loop – so that it can move freely.

If you were to simply tie it direct, the line would act a little like a damper and some movement of the lure would be absorbed – thereby restricting its movement.

The best, and most secure, knot to create a 'natural-movement' effect is the Rapala. So follow our step-by-step guide to help increase your catch rate by improving your lure presentation to the fish.

How To Tie The Rapala

Form an overhand loop, allowing six inches or so for the tag.

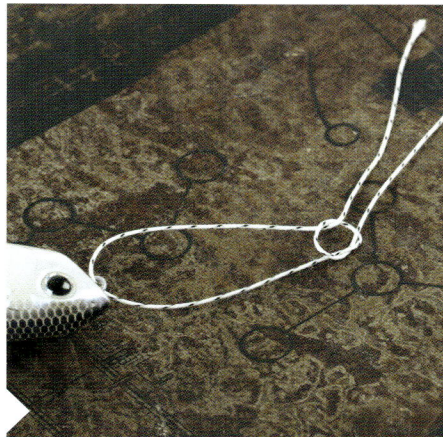

Pass the tag through the eye of the lure and back through the overhand knot.

Make three turns down the running line.

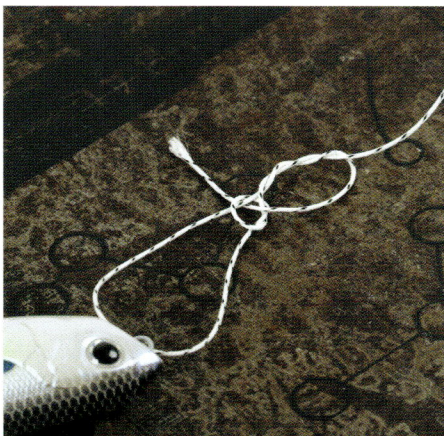

Pass the tag end through the overhand knot.

Now thread the tag end through the loop that you've just formed.

Lubricate with saliva, pull it all tight and trim the tag.

Words and pictures by Jim O'Donnell

Portlemouth Plaice

Catching specimen fish takes time and dedication. Jim O'Donnell follows ace angler Alex McDonald as he attempts to bag a big plaice.

Angler Profile

Name Alex McDonald
Where from Kingsbridge, Devon
Occupation Product and development manager for Red Gill Sakuma
Favourite fish Gilthead bream and rays
Most notable catch 45lb tope from the shore

There are plenty of shore marks to catch plaice throughout summer in south Devon, but they don't come more consistent than East Portlemouth on the Salcombe estuary.

I've known Alex McDonald from the Swift World Wide tackle company for many years and having fished with him on many occasions, there's one thing you quickly learn: he's a dedicated specimen hunter.

He targets particular species like clockwork throughout the year and like most good, big-fish anglers he puts in an awful lot of hours to achieve the results he craves.

While chatting to him, he revealed he was just starting his yearly campaign for a 3lb-plus plaice. I was instantly keen to follow him and try to record the event for TSF.

THE FISHING

Alex picked his position and set up his rod rest at the low water mark, the plan being to move back up the rocks as the tide flooded. Next he set up two rods: a pair of Zziplex M4 Evos paired with Daiwa's Millionaire 7HT Mag, loaded with 16lb Sakuma Nite Crystal line.

To each rod was tied either a two-hook loop rig or a single-hook drop-

East Portlemouth is a cracking venue with superb views.

down rig, which have often proved successful for Alex. Both are clipped-down rigs to help with distance and they present at least one bait below the lead, which is important when targeting flatties.

The drop-down rig is great if you're fishing on sand, but have to bring your fish in over rough ground, as it acts like a pulley rig.

SKILFUL MOVES

I love the way specimen anglers think deeply about their fishing and one of Alex's key tactics is to critically control the movement of his baits. Plaice are without doubt attracted by

About East Portlemouth

East Portlemouth is a small village five miles south of Kingsbridge and situated picturesquely on a raised area of land on the east side of Salcombe haven. Centuries ago it used to be a much larger and more flourishing place when it was a port and also an important ship-building centre.

It provided four ships and 90 men for the Crecy and Calais campaigns of 1346 and contributed at least one ship to chase the Spanish Armada in 1588. In 1879 the Duke and Duchess of Cleveland reorganised the whole village, with fishermen's cottages destroyed and farms disappearing.

There is an entrenchment visible on the hill, which was supposed to have been used when assaulting Salcombe Castle on the opposite side of the estuary.

The first plaice of the session weighed 1lb.

Top tips

Tides and movement
The plaice is quite an aggressive, predatory species. So adding a little movement to your bait can often help with attraction. Fish plain leads that will move around freely when there is little tidal movement, but grip leads when the tide is running hard.

Baits
Fish top-quality ragworm in clear-water conditions and don't be afraid to put two or three on the hook. If the water is in any way coloured, opt for smellier baits like lugworm and peeler crabs. Black lug and razorfish can also be effective.

Attractors
In clear conditions put a few small attractors above the hook to enhance the bait rather than as an outright attractor. Also consider using floating beads to add further movement to your baits.

Energy drinks
Most specimen angling is about putting in loads of time by the water. So staying alert is key. Energy drinks can be a real boost with this.

Doing time
Success comes with lots of dedication and time. So put in the effort and you will reap the rewards!

Size 1 or 1/0 hooks, swivels, attractors, beads, floating beads and links are all the terminal tackle you'll need to build rigs for plaice.

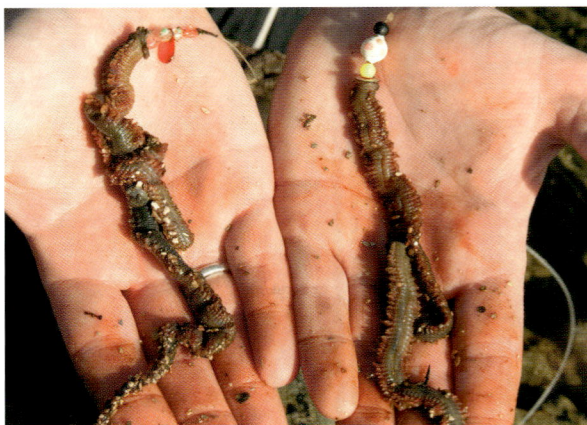

Large ragworm bait is Alex's favourite choice when fishing in clear water.

movement and Alex has found that when fishing ragworm baits in clear water, there's an optimum amount that you want the bait to move.

No movement in the bait at all or too much can result in very few takes. To control this, Alex fishes Breakaway 150g Impact grip leads when the tide is running hard, to pin them hard to the bottom. When the tide is at its weakest, he fishes the same leads, but without wires, in order to take full advantage of any extra movement that can be gained from the tide.

GIN CLEAR
For consistent fishing Alex likes gin-clear water when using ragworm with a few attractors. Two-thirds of his catches can be credited to a small floating bead just above the bait. If the water has the slightest colour, he switches to large lug and crab baits,

(sometimes several crabs on one bait), to add a little scent to attract them.

Plaice love crab and this is watercraft in its rawest form – it generally takes a big fish to swallow big baits, and a plaice that can gobble down five peelers is generally over 2lb! Alex uses Sakuma hooks for all of his plaice fishing, in the form of Sakuma 560 Stinger aberdeens in size 1 or 1/0. One thing Sakuma customers can be sure of is that Alex has rigorously tested every product the company sells and enjoys every moment of it!

IN SESSION
The tide wasn't running hard at the start of the session, so Alex opted for a plain lead, which he pendulum cast to 100 yards, putting the bait right out into deep water on the edge of the channel. I reckon it was maybe a bit over 20 feet deep. His second rod was

How To Find East Portlemouth

In Kingsbridge get onto the A379 eastbound and keep going through the villages of West and East Charleton. When you get to Frogmore, go through the village and near its end turn right over the bridge across the creek and head towards South Pool. From there on it's a single-track road all the way, going through South Pool with East Portlemouth regularly signposted along the way.

When you get to East Portlemouth, drive straight through the village until you reach the Mill Bay National Trust car park at the end of the road. Park up and from here follow the coastal path south for about half a mile through the woods, until you come across a large flat rocky area that gives way to shallow water and a sandy sea bed, adjacent to the Salcombe sand bar at the mouth of the estuary. All the way along this area produces good plaice fishing.

cast to the left, but a lot closer into shallower water. We then sat back and cracked open a couple of energy drinks, which Alex claims can play a big part in his angling.

He says: "It's all about being on the ball. I work 9am 'til 5pm and when conditions are perfect, I may fish four or five nights on the trot, so the energy drinks keep me focused on my rods."

Alex certainly needs something to give him a boost, because before I joined him for the plaice session, he had been targeting bull huss until the early hours – and was planning to target the species again after we had caught some plaice!

FIRST BITE

We'd only been looking at the rod tips for a few minutes when Alex reckoned he had a plaice on along with load of weed. He'd noticed the rod had weeded up earlier, but had left it fishing, knowing the bait would be still in prime condition.

He walked to the water's edge and slowly pumped in the weed. Hanging off the trace with the floating bead was a small plaice of just over 1lb. As soon as it was unhooked, he put it into a nearby rock pool so that it

could regain its strength before returning it.

An hour passed between bites. By this time Alex had moved back up the rocks with the incoming tide and switched to grip leads, which held his baits down in the current. Suddenly he hooked the second plaice of the session, which before being returned was estimated at a couple of ounces bigger than the first. Again, it fell to the trace with the floating bead.

DOUBLED UP!

His final casts of the day, before he headed off hussing for the night, were when the real action started. With both rods in position, he'd barely sat down when his rod at close range registered a small bite, followed by another. Plaice tend to hook themselves, so on the third bite he began winding and as soon as he felt the weight of the fish, he said it felt like a better one.

After gently pumping it in, he scrambled down the rocks to grab the fish, which turned out to be a

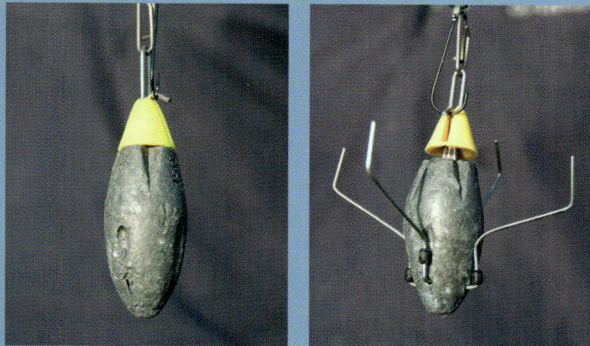

When the tide's not running, Alex uses plain leads to help add movement, but then moves on to a gripper as the tide picks up.

The second plaice of the day weighed just over 1lb and fell for the rag and floating-bead rig.

double header of decent plaice – both being very close to 2lb. This drew the short, but successful, session to a close. I was delighted it went well, but it hadn't been easy. It might appear we simply went out and caught our target species, but there were earlier trials and tribulations, which played out as follows…

THE HARD TIMES

For our first attempt we headed to a Torbay rock mark. Reports were that it had been throwing up good plaice for the past week and conditions were much the same. Things were looking good! But after a two-mile trek out to the headland, two anglers were already on Alex's favourite pitch, so we had to set up further along to the left.

Alex blanked while the two 'swim snatchers' caught three good-sized plaice and a bonus thornback. To make things worse, while I was out boat fishing the following week, Alex called me to say he was fishing with pals and they had caught more than 20 plaice between them, including his personal best of 3lb 6oz – Sod's Law!

Protect the future of your fishing.

Love your fishing? Then help us protect it. Angling is under threat from pollution, poaching, commercial over-fishing, restrictions to access, bad legislation and more...

Join us to unite all anglers, stand up for our sport, fight for its future and get people fishing!

Join the Angling Trust today
Call: 0844 77 00 616   www.anglingtrust.net

ANGLING
TRUST

The Two-Hook Seesaw Wishbone Rig

TSF reveals some of the best sea angling traces for you to use.

Although the 'wishbone' principle of fishing two hooks in close proximity to each other has been evident since the late 19th century, it wasn't until the early 1970s that the modern concept of the wishbone rig came into being. This evolved from the basic one-hook paternoster rig.

There are numerous wishbone designs currently used, but the simple seesaw is a good one to begin with as it is easy to tie, presents baits well, never tangles and is highly effective in all conditions.

For these reasons it's a regular match-winning rig for some of the top rods in the UK. It's also an essential rig for the casual angler, because it scores well with a wide variety of species by fishing two hook baits very close together at medium to long range.

How It Works

The reason the rig positions the Impact Shield within the 2in gap above the lead link is that it gives the Shield room to slide in. This movement means that the hook link won't stretch during a powerful cast. If the Impact Shield had no room to move, the hook link would stretch during casting and the hooks would then not sit tightly in the Shield for future casting.

The advantage of having the two hooks very close together is that the scent trail is stronger and more concentrated. This means that in fast tide runs the scent travels further before weakening. This offers the advantage of pulling fish in towards the baits from much further away. ▶

Build Sequence

Begin with a 42in length of 60lb rig-body line and tie on a lead link.

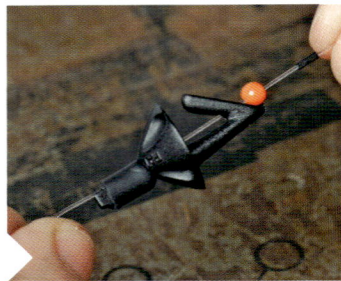

Slide on a Breakaway Impact Shield, a 5mm bead and a crimp. Fix the crimp in place two inches above the lead link.

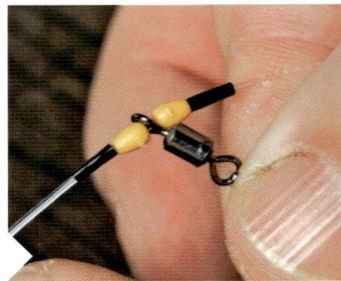

Slide on a rig crimp, followed by a 3mm rig bead, a size 6 rig swivel, another bead and a crimp. Be sure to leave these loose for now.

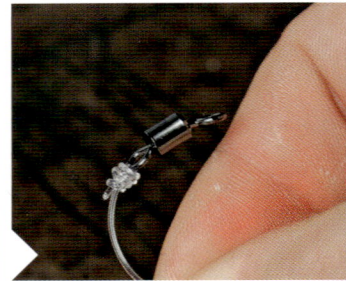

Tie on a size 4 rig-body connector swivel as the rig-to-leader connector.

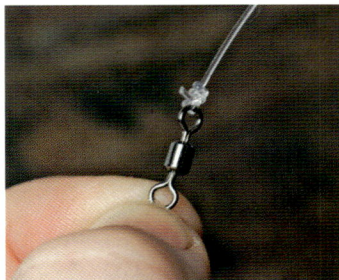

Take 24 inches of 60lb rig-body line and tie this to the size 6 rig swivel. This heavier, stiffer line will minimise tangles. Tie another size 6 rig swivel to the end of this 60lb line.

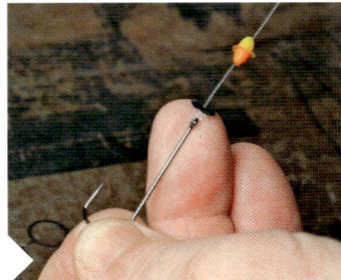

The hook-link line needs to be 20lb to 25lb, ideally fluorocarbon, but mono is okay, and about 26 inches long. Tie a size 2 Aberdeen hook at one end, slide on a sequin and a rubber rig stop.

Pass the free end of the line through the free eye of the swivel tied to the 60lb line, add another rubber rig stop, sequin, and tie on another hook. The rubber stops act as a sliding stop only, allowing the line to seesaw only so far before the rig stop jams up against the eye of the swivel.

Finish the rig by putting the hooks in the Impact Shield, then slide the main hook-snood swivel up the rig body until the hook snood comes just tight. Now crimp everything in place.

SWIVEL

CRIMP

SWIVEL

BEADS

CRIMP

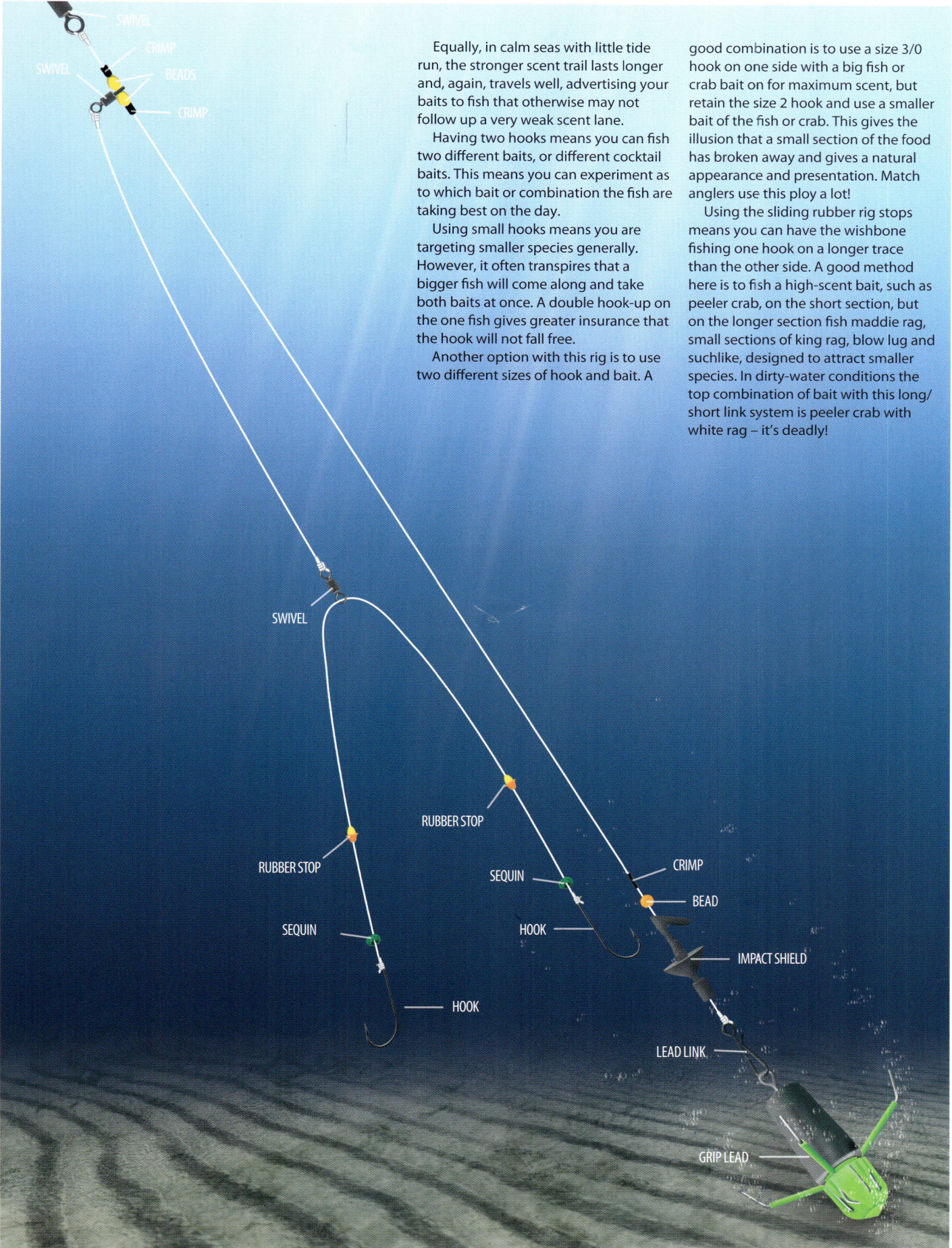

Equally, in calm seas with little tide run, the stronger scent trail lasts longer and, again, travels well, advertising your baits to fish that otherwise may not follow up a very weak scent lane.

Having two hooks means you can fish two different baits, or different cocktail baits. This means you can experiment as to which bait or combination the fish are taking best on the day.

Using small hooks means you are targeting smaller species generally. However, it often transpires that a bigger fish will come along and take both baits at once. A double hook-up on the one fish gives greater insurance that the hook will not fall free.

Another option with this rig is to use two different sizes of hook and bait. A good combination is to use a size 3/0 hook on one side with a big fish or crab bait on for maximum scent, but retain the size 2 hook and use a smaller bait of the fish or crab. This gives the illusion that a small section of the food has broken away and gives a natural appearance and presentation. Match anglers use this ploy a lot!

Using the sliding rubber rig stops means you can have the wishbone fishing one hook on a longer trace than the other side. A good method here is to fish a high-scent bait, such as peeler crab, on the short section, but on the longer section fish maddie rag, small sections of king rag, blow lug and suchlike, designed to attract smaller species. In dirty-water conditions the top combination of bait with this long/short link system is peeler crab with white rag – it's deadly!

SWIVEL

RUBBER STOP

RUBBER STOP

SEQUIN

SEQUIN

HOOK

CRIMP

BEAD

HOOK

IMPACT SHIELD

LEAD LINK

GRIP LEAD

Understanding
Anticyclones

David Hall explains how Mother Nature affects our angling…

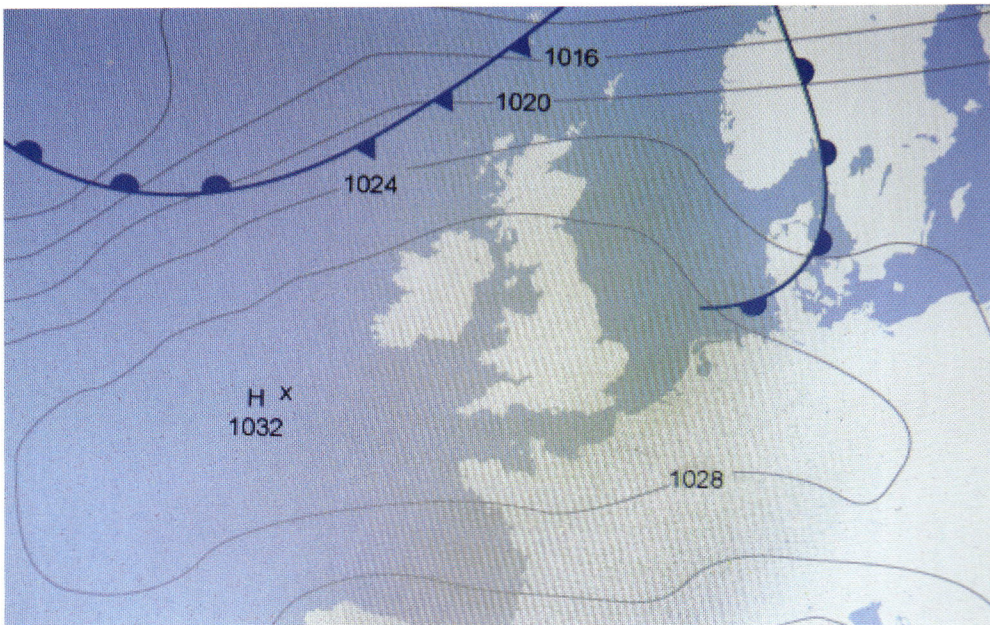

Weather charts are a mine of information once you've learnt how to read them.

The weather forecasts will often refer to anticyclones or high-pressure systems, and these are important for anglers to understand because they forecast light winds and calm seas, but can also predict fog and frost.

Anticyclones, unlike depressions, only have one type of air mass, but this covers a large geographical area and does not have either a warm or cold front. The area an anticyclone can cover is huge and can typically be in excess of 2,000 miles. Once an anticyclone becomes established it becomes dominant and can settle in over a large area and control the weather pattern for several days or more. The wind pattern will be light to calm and move clockwise around the centre of the anticyclone. This is shown on the weather charts by widely spaced isobars circling the centre of the anticyclone, with the pressure readings higher than 1,000 millibars.

Anticyclones are basically high-pressure systems, within which the air travels downwards in direction towards the earth's surface. As the air descends, the molecules become compressed and tightened, the pressure then increases and the air warms. When the air is warming, moisture in the atmosphere is evaporated, which means that no clouds can form, which produces clear, sunny skies and settled weather.

Here, in the UK, an anticyclone in mid-summer will mean very warm weather during the day with temperatures likely to be in the mid to high twenties of degrees Celcius. However, at night, and because there are no clouds to act as a shield, heat will quickly be lost.

The ground then cools, creating the condensation of water vapour in the descending warm air and causing heavy dew on the ground and mist. Both these will clear quickly come morning as the warmth from the sun's rays reheats the ground. After a few days of anticylonic weather, a layer of hot air builds up at ground level. This layer of hot air will eventually create thunderstorms, which will end the dominance of the anticyclone and change the weather pattern, freeing it from the anticyclone's influence.

During winter, though, the longer hours of darkness coupled with clear, cloudless skies create rapid cooling of the ground. With this there is a major risk of dew, frost and also thick fog patches, which can be persistent and slow to clear during the day. In very calm, windless conditions, the fog and frost can linger for several days or more. Air quality is also affected because, with little air movement, any air pollution is held at low levels, producing smog-like conditions.

Something else to watch out for is an anticyclone becoming anchored over northern Europe during winter. If this occurs, then most of the UK will be affected by very cold easterly winds that blow in from Siberia. These easterly winds tend to affect the fishing, with bites at a premium if the bitterly cold conditions persist – especially in the leeward areas of the west coast where the sea conditions will be flat and the water clarity rapidly turning gin clear. This especially applies to areas where the beaches are shallow, where light penetration through the clear water will push fish well offshore and make even night-time fishing difficult.

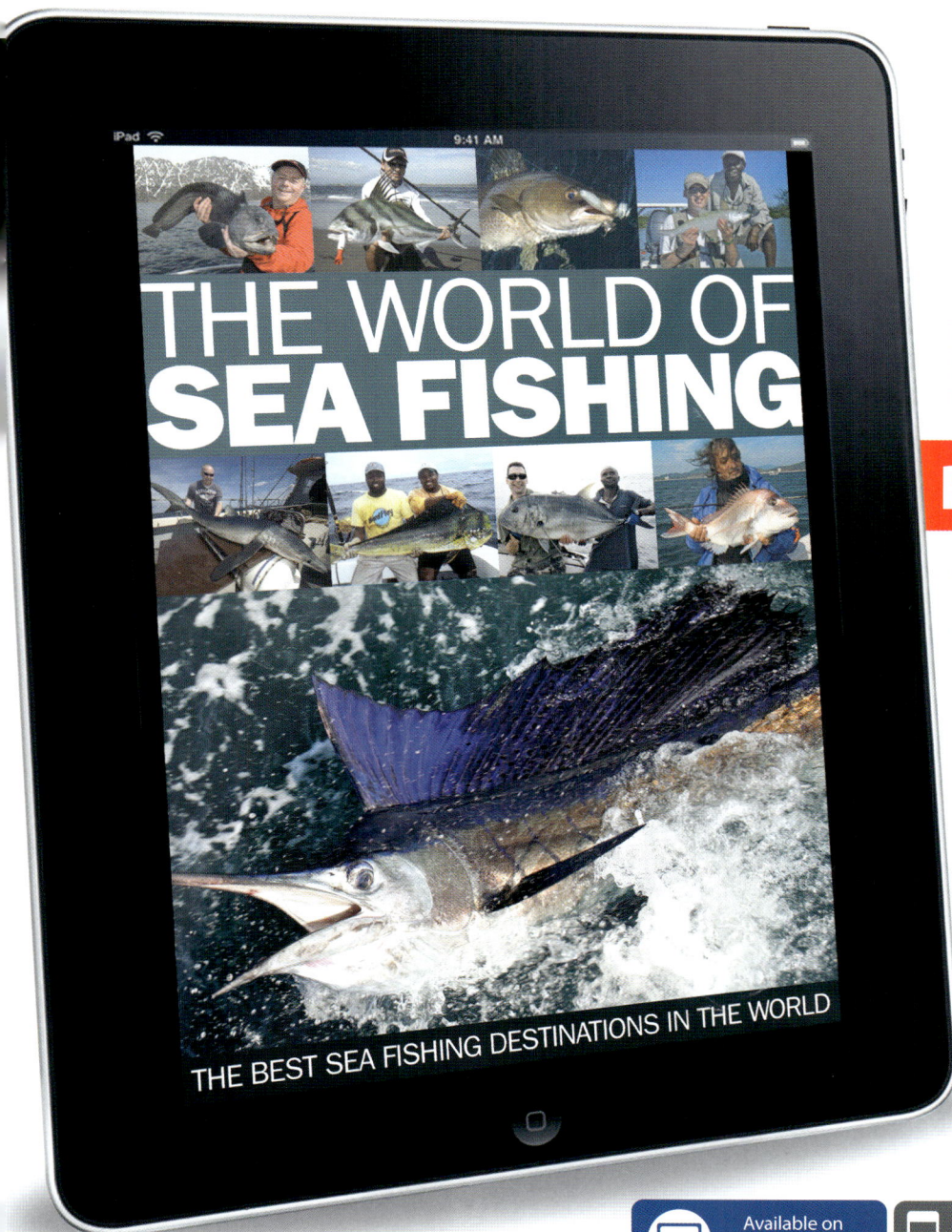

The Standard
Shockleader Knot

Be safe on the beach by learning how to tie a perfect shockleader knot.

There are immense forces involved during a cast, which put the line through extremely high stress. Casting a lead and bait on ordinary running line is ineffective because the line will simply snap, and the purpose of a shockleader line is to absorb this shock. For this purpose we use between 60lb and 80lb monofilament, which is tied direct to the running line.

There is, however, a rule of thumb that states a scale for leader strength to lead size, such as 50lb breaking strain for a 4oz sinker and add 10lb for every ounce extra above this. But, think about it, why not use 80lb for all general beach fishing? Then there can be no mistake.

The leader material can also readily handle the abrasion caused by sand, rocks and shingle, which is important because it's this line that mostly comes into contact with these objects.

By using a leader your confidence in casting and fishing will increase, as you'll be safe and have no fears of parting lines.

Top tips

Use saliva to lubricate the knot when tightening.

Make sure you have at least eight turns of leader line around the multiplier spool, or four for a fixed-spool reel.

Make the leader a minimum of one-and-a-half times the length of the rod you are using.

Try to trim tag ends as tight as possible so that they don't catch the rings or snag on the spool.

How To Tie A Shockleader

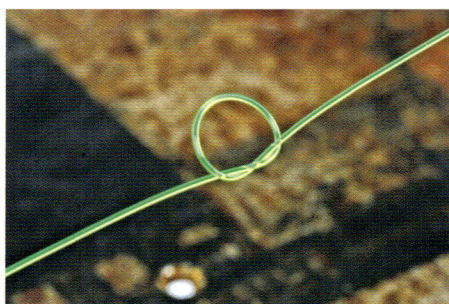
Form an overhand loop in the leader line, leaving plenty of tag.

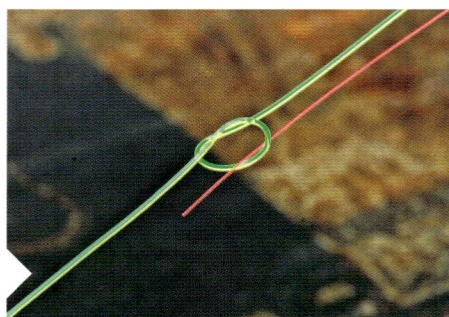
Pass the running line through the loop a few inches and in the direction pictured.

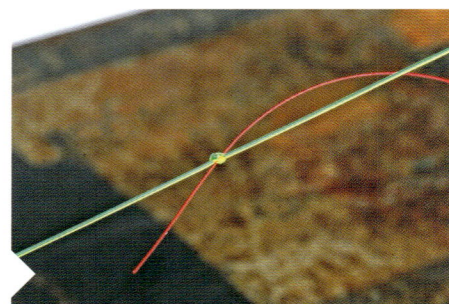
Pull the overhand loop as tight as you can, lubricate, and pull the running line through because this part will be slightly crushed and damaged.

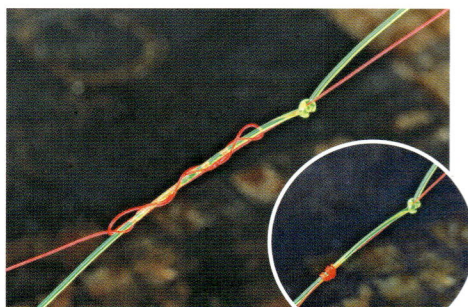
Form a uni knot with the running line, lubricate, pull up until nearly tight and bunch up the coils formed.

Moisten with saliva, slide the two knots together and then make a firm and steady pull. This tightens the whole knot down.

Trim the tag ends close and it's job done!

SAVE UP TO 20% ON THIS TOP ANGLING MAGAZINE

Summer Bream
On The
Ledge

Roger Mortimore hops aboard *Wight Sapphire* to do battle with some hard-fighting black bream on the Christchurch Ledge off the Dorset coast.

A couple of gentle taps turn into a bite that completely slams my rod tip over. Line is being ripped from the spool at an almighty rate as a hard-fighting fish dives for cover. I steel myself for the scrap ahead, my grip on the rod increases, muscles straining to hang on to the frenzy on the end of my line as beads of sweat run into my eyes. Slowly but surely, aided by the rod's action, I bring it under control. My wrist aches as I gain enough line to see a huge shape appear from the depths. "Look at the size of this," shouts skipper Bob Gawn as he slides the net under a huge black bream. Once on board it slams the scales down to 4lb 4oz and smashes my personal best! I have a huge smile on my face and I am so pumped with adrenaline that my hands are trembling and my legs are shaking.

Black bream are pretty fish, great fighters and good to eat.

BLACK BREAM Facts

- The British Boat Record for the black bream is a fish of 6lb 14oz 4dr caught by J A Garlick from a wreck off the South Devon coast that has stood since 1977.

- The British Shore Record is a massive 6lb 8oz 6dr taken in Creux Harbour, Sark, by R Guille in 2001.

- The black bream spawns in the spring between April and June. It matures as female when reaching 20 centimetres in length and may change sex to male at 30 centimetres. All bream over 40 centimetres long are male.

- It lays its eggs in nests and the male stays at the nest to guard the eggs until they hatch.

- The male black bream displays a brilliant blue on its head and fins during spawning.

- The black bream prefers rocky or rough ground and wrecks, feeding on small invertebrates, crustaceans, algae and small fish.

- Although the black bream can be caught at night, daytime is usually best.

- The black bream is common along the south coast, around the West Country and parts of the Welsh coast.

Venue

CHRISTCHURCH LEDGE

Wight Sapphire's former co-skipper Becki Florence finds time to enjoy some great action.

Roger readies himself for some top black bream fun.

I first met Bob and his former co skipper Becki Florence while visiting The Helm, a well-known hostelry in Westport, Co Mayo, during the 2008 Westport Skate Festival. Bob's boat *Wight Sapphire* was based at Yarmouth on the Isle of Wight. When Bob suggested that I join them on a trip out for black bream in the spring I jumped at the opportunity. I caught my first bream off Dartmouth, way back in the early 1970s. I was amazed at how hard these little fish fight all the way to the boat.

A date was selected just after Easter, when the tides were right and, hopefully, the weather would be settled for our outing.

After driving south through fog, I arrive at our pick-up point in Lymington in brilliant sunshine and no wind – perfect conditions.

After parking by the pontoon I meet fellow anglers Sean Nally, who has driven over from Hythe in Kent, and Matt Towgood from Southampton. Lymington is a regular pick-up point for Bob and handy for mainland-based anglers. Once all of our gear is loaded aboard we meet the other anglers, Owen Giles and Phil Smith. As we set sail Captain Becki points the bow of the boat toward the Christchurch Ledge.

We rig up ready for action as we travel along, some of the guys choose to use a single-hook running leger while the others opt for a one-up-

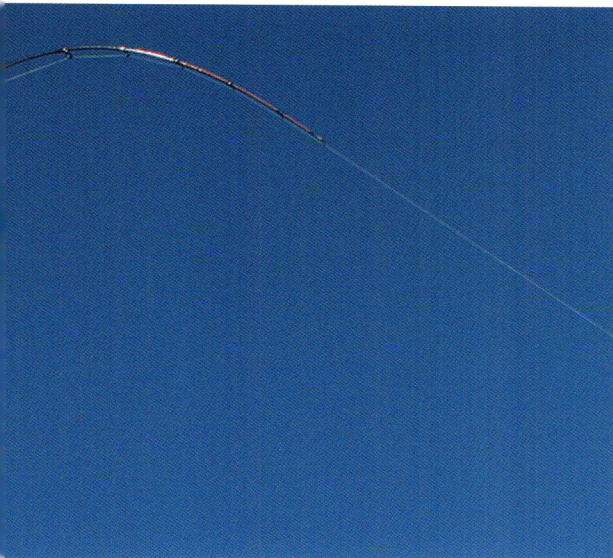

Bream Rig

Swivel ··········

9in snood ·······

Size 2 hook ·······

18in ·······

Boom ··········

9in to 12in snood ·······

3oz to 4oz lead ·······

Size 2 hook ··········

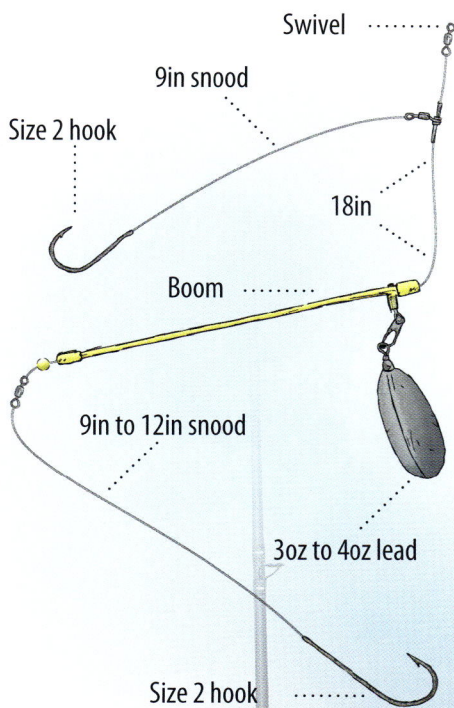

one-down rig, as bream often feed a few feet off the sea bed. Bream have small mouths, so small hooks are the order of the day. Our rigs are armed with size 4 and size 2 hooks baited with tiny strips of squid. Sean has a box of party squid – the little ones that are just a couple of inches long – and these are cut down the middle to make long, thin baits as they outfish a normal strip of squid by miles.

I rig up with a Fladen Super Sensor II rod; it's a little like a spinning rod that has soft fibreglass push-in tips. This will give me excellent bite indication and allow me to enjoy the fight of these feisty little fish. I match the rod with a Shimano Stradic3000 fixed-spool reel loaded with 15lb braid topped with 20 feet of fluorocarbon leader.

After a short steam we arrive at our mark and Bob drops anchor in the deep water just off the edge of the ledge. With more than 30 years of experience, Bob knows that the first shoals of bream tend to stay in the deeper water for a couple of weeks before they move up into the shallower water on top of the ledge. The flood tide we are fishing is a little disappointing with just nuisance dogfish and

pout but, suddenly, Sean is into a better fish that turns out to be a lively smoothhound that's taken his squid bait. A few minutes later and Sean is into another fish that's putting up a good scrap, but it's not a bream-type scrap and as it nears the surface we can see that it's a bass of around 2lb. We now have four species aboard, but where are the bream?

Bob explains they can be a little slow on the flood tide and that the ebb is usually more productive. We were about to find out how correct his advice was…

Slack water only produces a few more dogs, then skipper Bob shows the way by landing the first bream, a lively little female of around 1lb 8oz. I score next with a male fish around the same size as Bob's; the males are pretty fish with striking blue tinges on the head and fins. As the current picks up, so does the fishing and soon we are all having bites, but they are finicky and difficult to hit. The crew soon come to grips with hitting them, though, and Owen's spinning rod takes on a satisfying curve as he hooks his first bream of the session.

Southampton angler Matt Towgood cradles his PB bream of 3lb 9oz.

Hectic action saw three bream come aboard at the same time for Phil Smith, Bob Gawn and Roger.

Phil, Becki, Bob and I all hit into these hungry bream, but poor Matt had been missing bites until his rod suddenly bends double. This looks like a much better fish, and so it proves to be; it's a cracking personal-best bream for Matt at 3lb 9oz.

Everyone is buzzing now and catching regularly, the ebb is in full flow and has really put the bream on the feed, exactly as Bob predicted. All the small fish are returned to grow bigger with just a few of the better sized examples kept for a fish supper. I must have been into double figures in catch numbers when I spotted another bite. As I pick the rod up I feel another couple of taps then it just slams over and line peels off the spool. This is a much better fish and it's putting up a hell of a scrap; even at the back of the boat I have trouble lifting its head up so that Bob can net it. Eventually it's safely in, my trembling hands remove the hook and it's a new personal best for me. I have to sit down and compose myself, my hands are shaking so much that I can't bait up again for a while.

Unfortunately, the 60 tiny squid in Sean's box soon run out as his squid soon became 'our' squid, so we decide to call it a day and head for home. Perfect conditions and great banter on a glorious spring day and we've all caught plenty of fish. Isn't this what it's all about? Isn't this the feeling that we all go fishing for?

Top tips

The black bream has a small mouth so use hooks in sizes 6, 4 or 2 and match your bait size to the hook that you're using. The top baits are small strips of squid, mackerel or sandeel and tiny pieces of peeler crab. A tiny squid mounted on a size 2 Aberdeen is perfect.

Despite its small mouth, the black bream has some good strong teeth so use snoods of 15lb or 20lb breaking strain to avoid being bitten off.

Use light gear where you can to gain the best sport possible from this great little fighter.

The black bream can be a finicky feeder, giving very gentle bites, so using a tiny bait on a very sharp size 6 hook will help convert bites to fish landed.

If you still miss the bites, try using braid; its lack of stretch will hit those sneaky bites better.

When the current dies down, the black bream may feed up off the sea bed, so try using sandeel feathers with size 6 or 8 hooks baited with tiny pieces of squid or mackerel.

The black bream spawns in the spring, so try to return most of your fish so that they have chance to reproduce.

INFORMATION

Wight Sapphire is an Offshore 105, powered by a Daewoo 360hp diesel engine. She's licensed to carry eight passengers (COP Cat 2). *Wight Sapphire* has all the up-to-date navigation equipment, including coloured GPS, depth sounder, radar and DSC radio. All the safety equipment needed is stowed on board. There's also a portable toilet!
If you'd like to fish around the Isle of Wight, give Bob a call on 01983 740554 or on his mobile on 07967 910565
E-mail: wightsapphire.charters@talktalk.net
Website: www.wightsapphireboatcharters.co.uk

Roger's over the moon with his new PB 4lb 4oz bream.

Part of the action.

The new echoMAP series comes ready to hit the fishing action with you. An amazing chartplotter and fishfinder combination fearuring BlueChart® g2 maps capability, Garmin advanced HD-ID™ sonar technology, wireless connectivity and built-in high-sensitivity 10Hz GPS receivers that update your position and heading 10 times per second – dramatically improving your ability to mark and navigate right to waypoints. Available with 7″ WVGA pinch-to-zoom touchscreens or 5″ VGA displays. Advanced technology made easy to use. It is truly the power of simple.

GARMIN®

To learn more go to garmin.co.uk

Blow Lugworm

Shore angling expert Alan Jeffrey shows you how to find, dig and keep your own blow lugworms (*Arenicola marina*).

Over the years, I've dug thousands of lug and found that the art of extracting them from the sand and mud is a very easy and satisfying activity.

By following several self-taught procedures, I've been able to spare my back from many of the pains inflicted after an hour's dig for one of the UK's most common shore worms.

Lug is the most commonly used sea bait in the UK and, also, one of the most expensive. On average the majority of sea anglers usually pay as much as £3.50 a score, and when buying five score at a time, this can become a very expensive outlay every time you go fishing. Just imagine that you go fishing once a week – the lug

bought would equate to around £910 a year – and just imagine the amount of quality angling equipment you could buy with that money. You could even subscribe to the UK's top angling magazine TSF for the next 20 years and still have plenty of change left!

I completely understand that, with work commitments, many anglers are unable to collect their bait, but I also know many anglers who simply can't be bothered, so they just order them from the nearest bait supplier.

I find this hard to understand because lug can be one of the easiest baits to collect at any time of the year. Even after a heavy night's frost in the winter months or during spring or summer storms, lug can be very easy to extract from

the mud and sand – plus I find that it's quite a therapeutic pastime.

Blow lug, as they're commonly known, can be found on most open sandy beaches. They usually live in very large colonies with hundreds and, at times, thousands occupying a small area of the foreshore. Lug are also normally found just below the high watermark, so you don't need to venture out as far as you would if you were collecting their larger cousins – blacks and yellowtails.

When digging blow lug, much depends on the nature of the ground and the concentration of casts. The easiest digging is where there are lots of close casts in soft ground. When you come across these types of worm beds, an old trusty potato

When there are many worm casts, simply dig the area over at one or two fork depths to find the worms.

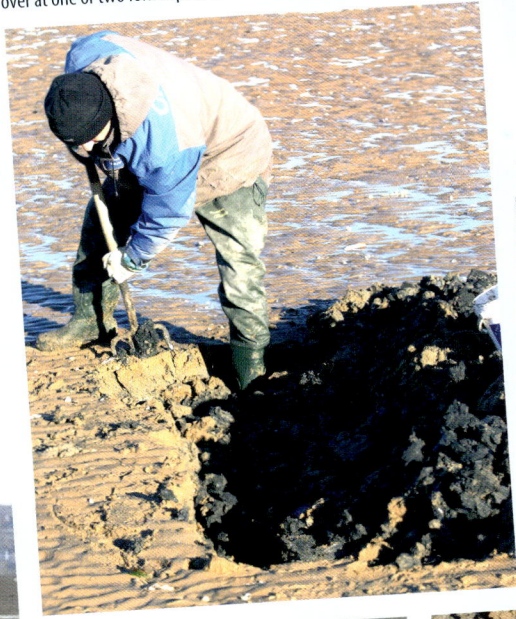

It's a common sight to see bait diggers at work when the tide is out. Here, Alan can be seen digging a trench to dry an area that he'll dig for lugworms.

The water drains into the trench.

fork is ideal, and the method that I use to dig this type of terrain is commonly known as 'trenching'. This is where you pick an area with lots of casts and dig it over – a little like turning the soil in your garden.

The secret of successful trenching is to keep the hole clear and water free, and as you dig back over your chosen ground you'll start to pick up the worm as it becomes exposed – you must be quick because they can attempt to burrow again.

With a little understanding you can start to learn and anticipate the location of the worms, which means that you can reduce the chances of damaging them with the fork.

If the region to be dug is covered in a shallow level of water, which you'll often find in many open mudflats and estuaries, it's easy to dig a low channel around a good bit of ground to drain the water off before digging.

In many areas, depending on which part of the coastline you live, the worms burrow in fairly hard ground and are often spread well apart – these will have to be dug individually.

There's a very easy technique to this that involves digging along an imaginary line between the cast and the blowhole. Start the dig just before the cast and deepen the hole to the depth that you think the worm is likely to be found. Keep the hole visible and follow the worm cast until the tail of the worm can be seen. At this point remove as much sand or mud as possible then push the fork deeply in front of the worm, levering out this section of sand with the worm in it.

The same practice can be used on soft sand but there's another method that I've used successfully and it's from my very first days of collecting my own bait. With this method you use the trenching fork

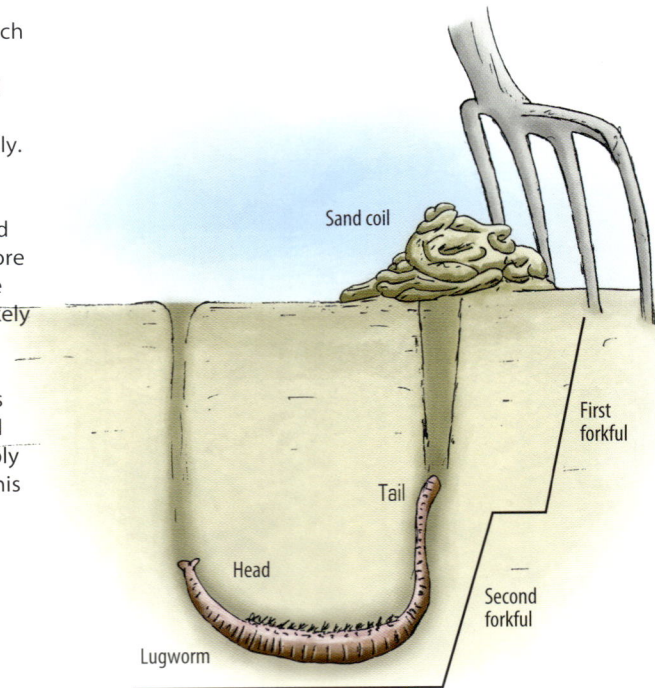

Sand coil

First forkful

Tail

Head

Second forkful

Lugworm

Keep the worms in a centimetre of fresh sea water in a cat-litter tray – only 10 to 20 at a time.

Now, like in the picture, keep the worms in a fridge and ensure that the fridge is at a constant temperature between 5°C and 10°C.
Check regularly for dead or dying ones and remove them. You can identify these by seeing if the water has dirtied or changed to a bloody colour – be sure to replace the water immediately from sea water stored in the same fridge! Now wrap up these dead worms and use them straightaway or freeze them for another day.

Or...

Lay the clean, dry lug in a straight line on fresh newspaper.

Start to roll them up so that they remain straight.

Once you have 20 or so wrapped up, seal over the ends of the paper. This way the lug stay in top condition for when you put them onto the hook.

or a normal spade and, again, use the make-believe line between the cast and the blowhole as your point.

Dig a shallow trench next to the line but about eight inches to one side. This shallow channel should extend the full distance between the cast and the blowhole and be a little deeper than the expected worm's depth.

Next, sink the spade deeply in to the other side of our make-believe line to the trench – the best place is halfway between cast and the blowhole.

Then cautiously lift the sand out of the hole – hopefully without breaking it up – and you'll find that, most the time, the worm should be in the sand.

This isn't an exact science but if you practise and master this technique, it will require far less effort.

Looking after blow lug is just as important as digging for them. When you've collected your bait, cleaning the undamaged lug is essential. Place the lug in a bucket and pour small amounts of sea water over them, separating them from the sand and mud as you go. Repeat this process a couple of times and then place the worms in clean sea water for the transfer back home.

However, don't disregard the broken or damaged lug – place them on paper and let them dry out. In the past these broken worms have been as productive as the undamaged ones; they're also extremely effective when the dabs are in residence or when you're flounder fishing.

When storing the lug, regulating the thermometer on the fridge is one of the most important things to do. I never store them in temperatures lower that 5°C and no higher than 10°C. By keeping the worms between these two temperature points, I've been able to keep them fresh for well over month.

WEATHER EFFECTS

Anticipate the blow lug to move deeper in to the sand or mud during periods of hard frosts. This is the one time when the digging may be more industrious during

This is what you want – a nice big juicy lug!

Collect any dug worms in a bucket of sea water.

ebb tides because the worm beds are just uncovering and the sand and mud have been warmed by the water.

Over the years, all of my best digs have come during heavy rainstorms and I have my own theory why this is. I believe that the amount of rainwater seeping into the burrow and sand tricks the worm into thinking the tide is flooding.

VARIATION IN TIDES

I tend to dig the two tides either side of the largest tides of the month. The obvious reason is that you can have more time over your favoured digging grounds.

This can vastly affect the collection of lug because the worms have a tendency to go deeper while the tide is still ebbing. Almost immediately as the new tide starts to flood, the worms will rise in the sand making them easier to dig.

GROWTH AND REPRODUCTION

Many lug spawn together into the sea at the same time in the autumn and the larvae stay near the sea bed where they develop into adults. Scientists who have studied this species believe they can live as long as 10 years and they very rarely move far from their birth area.

They eat the sand and mud that falls in to the top of their burrow, digesting the small pieces of plant and other food in them – the waste forms the worm casts.

At the height of the tide, the head of the lug will face towards the open end of the burrow and it will go lower in the burrow as the water level goes down, moving until it's at the very bottom. The lug uses the hairs on the side of its body, combined with pulsing waves through its body, to move in the burrow.

Lug stay in their burrows and don't move until breeding in autumn when they'll make new burrows and release their eggs or sperm into the sea water, which is where they fertilise. Young lug then hatch and create their own burrows generally higher up the tide line, moving down as they mature.

They grow up to 20 centimetres long and live in the bottom of a U-shaped burrow. They line the walls of their burrows with sticky mucus to stop them collapsing and to keep a current of water moving through to provide oxygen.

Lug digging, to me, is an autumn and winter activity; during the late spring and summer months I concentrate mainly on other types of baits, unless I'm boat fishing in deeper waters.

I know of many individuals who collect lug all-year round and they have some excellent angling adventures, but I start my lug excavations when my friends who own or work on the local trawlers inform me that the whiting and cod are starting to show.

Top tips

Never open your fridge during stormy conditions because the sudden change in air pressure will result in many lifeless lug.

Always keep a container of fresh sea water in the fridge and never use sea water that's been allowed to warm up on the garage or shed floor.

Only store up to 20 worms in a tray at any one time; keeping them thinned out in this way will help you keep them for longer periods of time.

Dry the worms on several pieces of newspaper for a couple of hours and only wrap them in fresh paper before you decide to go fishing.

I never wrap the lug in the same way as they do when you buy them from a bait supplier. I always roll them individually because I've found you get a better presentation as you slide them onto the hook.

Congers In The Spotlight

Clumsy Simon Everett accidently dropped a navigation light overboard, only to enjoy some illuminating action.

The conger is one of the iconic species for anglers to target because it offers the chance – even for people fishing from the shore – to do battle with a big, hard-fighting fish. I can still envisage the sight of an eel nudging the 80lb mark that was caught from the harbour wall at Mevagissey, Cornwall, in the 1970s!

For the experienced kayak angler, congers present a real challenge and one that is certainly magnified at night, but so too are the chances of hooking one. When targeting large, hard-fighting fish such as conger eels from a kayak it is not just the tackle that has to be well prepared; the angler has to be properly equipped with full safety kit and the ability to handle both the kayak and the power of a very angry fish in the dark.

There are several spots around Britain's shoreline – especially in the southwest – where fearsome congers can be landed from kayaks but one of the best is nestled along Dorset's Jurassic Coast.

Lulworth Cove near the village of West Lulworth receives a staggering one million tourists each year, who flock down to gaze at the spectacular natural bay before heading off to the famous rock arch at nearby Durdle Door. What few of these holiday-makers realise about Lulworth Cove, however, is that it offers, nay virtually guarantees, the chance of hooking a conger.

After checking that the weather was perfect, and that there was a neap tide, I and two pals, Paul Fennel from Chandlers Ford and Dave Tratt from Southampton, headed for Dorset to do battle with the serpents of the sea that lurk in the magnificent rock formations.

This was my first visit to the mark but Paul and Dave assured me that there was a very good chance of catching some rod-bending congers. They had been several times before and had successful trips by studying the local

SUCCESS! Dave Tratt holds aloft a 35lb-plus conger taken in just 40 feet of water at night.

When targeting congers it doesn't pay to go too light because they put up mighty fights and will test tackle to the limit. A multiplier loaded with 50lb braid is normally matched to a rod in the 20lb to 30lb class. Congers don't have sharp teeth but they are capable of biting through thin monofilament just the same so my hooklength was made up of 80lb mono to a Sakuma Manta Extra 6/0 hook. I had a secret weapon for my weight, a luminous Norwegian pirk with the hook removed, just threaded on as a sliding weight and with just an 18in hooklength so that my bait was close to the luminous attractor. The others were similarly equipped, except they had stronger hooklengths consisting of 150lb mono.

charts in detail and using their fishing brains to work out where the congers would be.

Night fishing from a kayak needs a little more preparation than normal and we were all equipped with a headtorch each and a white navigation light in addition to the normal safety gear. Our camping kit was stowed in the hulls ready

We set off from the sheltered harbour at Lulworth Cove just as the sun was starting to cast long shadows and throw an orange blanket over everything. The cliffs glowed against the blue sky and the kayaks stood out as silhouettes against the shimmering sea.

We needed to catch bait and just outside the cove there is an upwelling formed by the rocks. If you can find this spot it can be relied on to produce mackerel, which is probably the finest conger bait available.

With the sea's surface flat calm it was easy to see the line of demarcation where the water was diverted upwards and we were soon unhooking mackerel from our Sabikis. Tratty got some tiny pollack, too, but they were far too small to be of any use. After half an hour we had plenty of mackerel and headed off to the mark while there was still light in the sky.

The mark is very specific. It's a spot where an underwater geological fault creates an overhang in the rock and the congers follow the base of this submerged cliff. Paul discovered it one day by closely studying the contours and using his fishfinder to locate the drop-off.

Tratty kept station on the mark by paddling against the tide while I dropped anchor and paid out line to hold the kayak over the spot before the other two dropped anchor about 20 yards either side of me.

It may seem that we were all very close together but congers don't tend to put in long, searing runs, preferring to battle it out in the vertical plane, so there was little chance of us tangling.

We all lay to the gently flowing tide while starting to prepare our baits when disaster struck – I knocked my navigation light overboard! It was supposed to be attached by a lanyard, but the loop of the lanyard came off as well and my Tektite plunged to the sea bed, directly under my kayak.

We were only in about 40 feet of gin-clear water and every now and then I could clearly see the wand

lying on the bottom, emitting its bright, white light. I cursed myself for being so stupid, because it was brand new, but then I recalled a skipper having once told me that he often attached a waterproof torch to a line and lowered it to the bottom as a technique to attract congers. He swore by the method but there was only one difference between his ploy and mine – he could retrieve his torch when he had finished. Mine was lost for good and shows the importance of ensuring that everything is securely attached to the kayak.

With half a mackerel on the 6/0 hook I lowered my luminous weight to the bottom, set the lever drag very light and put the ratchet on. The others did the same.

Within five minutes I got a couple of strong nods on the rod and the line started to peel off the reel as the ratchet clicked. I gave it a few seconds, then pushed the lever drag forward to the strike position and lifted. At the same time I started to crank the handle and managed to get the conger off the bottom before it knew what was happening. I regained about 20 feet of line before the conger really woke up and pulled back with an immense surge of power.

I could feel the power of the fish rippling through the rod as the tip ring bent right over and touched the water. My 20lb/30lb-class rod was bent almost into a semicircle and the fish was still pulling some line off the reel. Then –

ping – it all went slack. I wound in to find that my 80lb hooklength had been bitten through.

I made up another trace, this time using some 150lb mono, and baited another 6/0 hook with half a mackerel. This was sent down into the eerily glowing depths beneath the kayak where the Tektite light was still glowing brightly. The glow from the torch was obviously helping to attract congers, which can be quite curious because my bait hadn't been down more than a minute or so when the ratchet on my reel once more alerted me to the line going out.

Once again I put the drag on and lifted into the fish, winding fast to gain as much line as possible before the eel could react and try to dive for any underwater obstructions. But suddenly the eel gave one mighty lunge just as I felt I had things under control and it was gone.

Examining the end of the line showed that the braid had been chafed on a rock.

Although it was now 2-0 to the congers, the heartening thing about the session was discovering that the light which I had accidently dropped overboard was doing a good job because the others hadn't had so much

Angler Profile

Name: Dave Tratt
From: Eastleigh, Hampshire
Occupation: Builder
Best fishing: Bream on light gear
Best fish: A 50lb tope from a kayak
Years fishing: Longer than he can remember!

Tratty brings his conger to the kayak. With its head out of the water, the big eel goes very docile; they often do after their initial surface spinning antics.

Tackle for conger fishing at night: a whole mackerel fished on a Sakuma Manta Extra 5/0 hook. The 8oz luminous pirk used as a weight is an added attraction to the bait fished on a short running-leger rig.

The Tektite wand used for Si's mast light that went overboard.

as a knock.

Tratty decided to anchor closer to me and put a fresh bait down. He was now much nearer to the submerged light and, to show just how great the pulling power of the beam appeared to be, within minutes of his fresh mackerel hitting the bottom he was bent into a good eel.

Tratty's builder's hands cranked the eel into mid-water before it decided that it wanted to be deeper and took line off his reel as it fought against the drag and arched the rod. The hook held firm, as did the 150lb trace, and a few minutes later it broke the surface beside his kayak only to start spinning round like a rubber band on a model aircraft, sending spray flying in all

directions. Hauling on the trace, Dave pulled the thrashing eel over the side of his kayak, keeping its head well up. As soon as he had it out of the water the eel calmed down, the thrashing stopped and it went limp.

Dave held it aloft for a trophy shot although we didn't weigh it; rather we compared its thickness with Tratty's second-row-forward's thighs and judged that its head was nearly the same size as the big man's, so we estimated it to be at least 35lb.

With photographs having been taken to confirm the capture, Dave took his T-bar and unhooked the magnificent fish so that it could be released back into the depths with the minimum of fuss.

That was the last fishing action of the night, so with the tide easing off, and the fact that it was approaching 1am and we still had to set up camp back on shore, we decided to up anchor and make our way to the beach for a brew and put our heads down for the night. Although we had only landed one conger, the session had still provided plenty of excitement and showed why more people than ever are having a crack at kayak fishing.

Also, accidentally dropping the light over the side and seeing how well the mishap worked in attracting fish to the area was also pretty illuminating. I shall certainly be trying the tactic again… but with the light FIRMLY secured on a line next time.

The Palomar Knot

Learn a quick, strong and effective way to attach lines to terminal tackle.

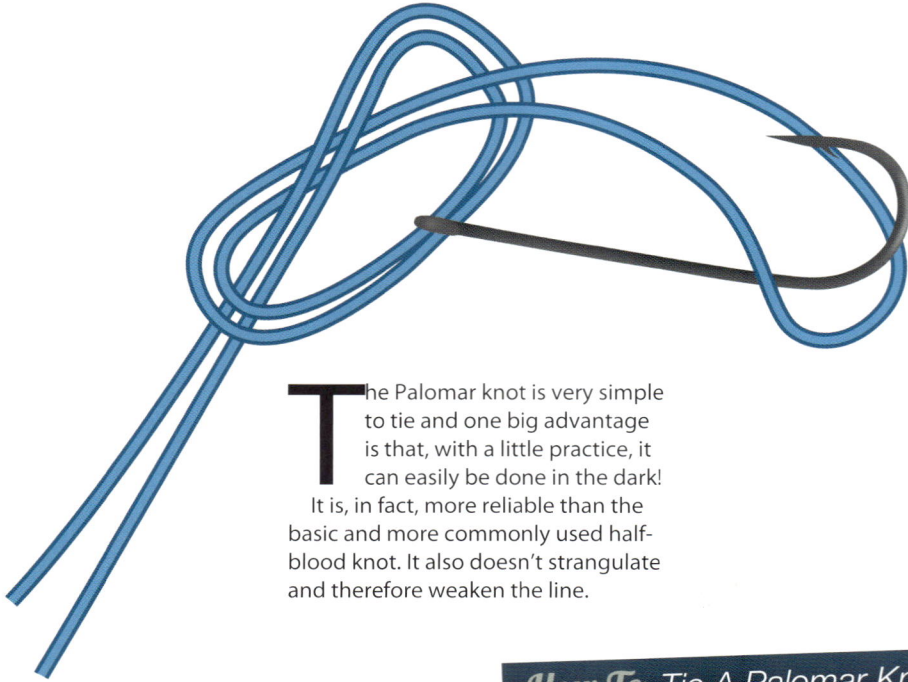

The Palomar knot is very simple to tie and one big advantage is that, with a little practice, it can easily be done in the dark! It is, in fact, more reliable than the basic and more commonly used half-blood knot. It also doesn't strangulate and therefore weaken the line.

Top tips

Ensure that the loop you form is long enough to pass around the bend of the hook.

Always use saliva to lubricate when you tie knots.

Use pliers to hold the hook shank as you tighten the knot.

How To Tie A Palomar Knot

Form a loop in the line and pass it through the eye of the hook or swivel.

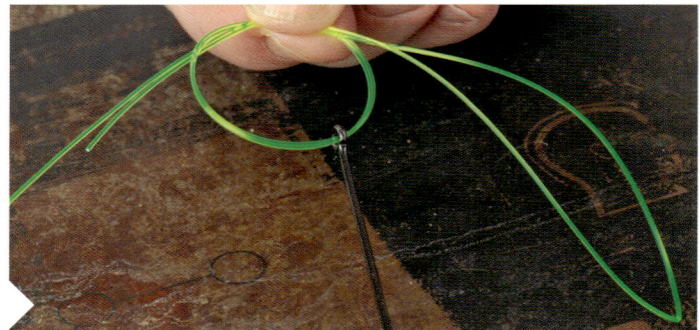

Form an overhand knot in the loop of line.

Pass the loop end over the bend of the hook.

Pull the knot tight . . . and it's finished.

Understanding
Brackish Water

David Hall explains how Mother Nature affects our fishing…

Freshwater will enter the sea via rivers and streams running from the mainland.

The effects of freshwater mixing in with saltwater dramatically influences the way estuary and inshore species behave. The consequences are important for anglers to understand in order for them to maintain and maximise their catches.

Sea water is obviously rich in salt, whereas freshwater contains far fewer dissolved salts and is therefore less dense. When the two waters mix the effect will be that the saltwater will be diluted by virtue of the reduction in salt content due to the influx of freshwater. This change in the salt content occurs where freshwater streams or small rivers meet beaches. The more freshwater-tolerant species, such as bass and flounders, may be attracted to this freshwater entry point. But other open-sea species, such as dabs and whiting, will tend to avoid the immediate proximity of this inflowing freshwater and are likely to be found uptide or at a distance seaward where the salt content of the water is unaffected, or at least much less diluted.

Estuaries are less easy to figure out. In some deeper estuaries, when saltwater and freshwater meet, stratification or layering can occur. This simply means that the two water types do not mix and remain, to a large extent, separated. The freshwater, being less dense than the saltwater, floats over the top of the saltwater. This tells us that any incoming sea fish will stay in the saltwater level only and close to the sea bed, so leger fishing will be the most effective technique at such times.

Deep fjords with dominant river outflows and less tidal motion often have this kind of water layering and can also have a layer of cold, stagnant, water with poor nutrition just above the floor of the fjord. Fish life here will be minimal. Anglers who have fished

Norway will know that in these deep-water fjords, the best of the fishing is generally over ground within 20 to 70 metres of the surface. Much deeper water tends to only see torsk and the odd wolf-fish caught as a result of this cold-water band.

In larger estuaries, such as the Thames and Bristol Channel, the effects of freshwater are minimised, and the fishing during times of heavy rainfall will not be overly affected. However, there may be a movement outwards by fish from the headwaters to water that is more salt heavy. In these conditions expect the mid to seaward marks to produce the best fishing.

In smaller estuaries, at times of low rainfall, fish such as bass and flounders will penetrate right to the junction of freshwater. But when heavy acidic floodwater from moors or mountains is pouring down through the estuary, even the flounders and bass will fall back, with the seaward end of the estuary likely to be the only area to provide some fishing, and even then only once a new flood tide has pushed in in some way and raised the salt content back to acceptable levels.

Also take note of any small feeder streams alongside the estuary flanks. If one side has more feeder streams than the other, predominantly saltwater fish, such as flounders and bass, will tend to run the side of the estuary where the saltwater content mix is highest. This can often be seen as a definite demarcation line of brown floodwater and grey-coloured seawater. Even mullet will avoid dirty-brown acidic floodwater and seek out areas where salt dilution and waterborne clarity are greater.

This demarcation line of saltwater and floodwater can also be seen inshore along shallow surf beaches after prolonged heavy rain. Using any high ground to visually identify areas where the brown floodwater effect is lessened can see you catch fish when fishing would otherwise be pointless.

Mussel beds hold plaice and flounders.

We show you how to identify areas in estuaries that will be holding fish so that you can improve your catch rate!

Find The Features,
Find The Fish

Estuaries are best described as fish highways. Fish, such as bass, mullet, cod and coalfish, travel down the main and side channels, stopping to feed at food-holding stations along the way. The fast tide runs associated with estuaries help the fish cover the maximum amount of ground, plus the feeding can be rich and varied giving a high return of calories for the expenditure of very little effort.

To get the best from estuary fishing we need to be able to read exactly where these food stations are and anticipate when the fish will be there. It's a simple equation of right place, right time.

The problem is that not all the estuary uncovers at low tide. Much will still be covered by water, so we need to learn to read, if possible, where fish hotspots might be.

SMALL ESTUARY BARS
Bass especially will wait just before low water out beyond the main channel sand bar, which can usually be seen at low tide as short surf tables breaking over shallow sand between the flanks of the channel. As the flood tide begins the bass come with the tide and into the main channel proper. Knowing this means you can ambush the fish as they initially enter the estuary.

Inside the estuary mouth, if the main channel is fairly shallow, look where the main tide run flows. You will often find seed mussel beds here, which will hold bass as they move through with the tide, but also big flounders and plaice. These areas can fish well either side of low water, but tend to fish best during slack water either side of high tide.

THE MAIN CHANNEL
The middle of the main channel will hold flatfish. It's a common mistake, though, to make long casts into the channel as the tide floods. Better fishing is found by casting short into the surf and onto shallowing ground that

The flounder is a prime target species in small estuaries.

Gullies separated by sandbanks will hold food such as sandeels, and bass, turbot, plaice and flounders will feed here.

Where there's a steep bank at your feet is good for bass.

the tide floods onto as it spills out from the main channel. All manner of food such as shrimps, worms, shellfish and crabs are exposed as the tide floods in, and bass, turbot and flounders will work right on the tide-line edge looking to feed.

If you can find slightly deeper hollows, small sandbank areas and little gullies, then these will be the real hotspots as the fish pass through. You can identify these by using a light plain lead and after casting out let the bait roll round with the tide until it stops. This is where much of the natural food will find a resting place, and so too will the fish.

Often you can see shallow areas where the channel is split into two, separated by sandbanks. The inclines of these banks are brilliant for holding flounders, plaice, turbot if the banks are located towards the mouth of the estuary, and also bass will work them looking for sandeels as the tide floods.

If you find areas where a narrowing main channel cuts in close to a steep bank at your feet, this can be a good place to fish for bass, but for flounders a long cast onto the far bank where the water is shallower and

slower will give a better catch.

Look to see if the main channel really bottlenecks or narrows quickly anywhere – this will concentrate the tide flow more strongly. The faster tide flow will dig out a deeper hole here, and this can hold flounders, plaice, sometimes dabs and good bass. In winter small coalfish, whiting and good codling can often be caught in these holes too. Any food washed along by the tide naturally falls here and holds the fish.

Often where the tide bottlenecks you will find areas of rougher ground and weed. These hold crabs and small fish and, as the tide floods through this and the water deepens, the bass come in to work – quartering the ground, scaring out food as they go. These marks often flood from about mid-tide on and can fish well right up to high water and maybe the first hour of the ebb.

During the bigger spring tides towards mid-flood when the flow is strongest, you will often see seagulls and terns feeding on sandeels, with the bass splashing the surface as they make a kill. You can cast spinners or a frozen or artificial sandeel worked behind a float through

Mullet are regular visitors to the estuary system.

Feed is held on the ropes or chains attached to mooring and channel buoys and on the sea bed where they're anchored. These buoys or markers also identify the deepest part of the channel for boats as they navigate the river.

this tide-run area, and it can fish extremely well.

As the main channel runs further into the estuary, look for areas where the estuary flanks are weedy and rocky. These areas fish well with crab baits cast just a few yards out for bass either side of high water. The bass come in looking for crabs, shannies and butterfish and again catches can be excellent if you find the right mark.

ROUND THE BEND

Bends in the route of the main channel are always hotspots. Never fish on the wide side of the bend where the tide flow is strongest. Flounders, and sometimes plaice, tend to hold up on the inside of the bend and just rearwards from the actual corner. Here the tide flow is broken by the inner edge of the bend, but food is pushed in by the tide and deposited in the slacker water. The flatfish can sit on the edge of this current and pick off food as it passes by.

Bass are different. They swim with the tide flow on the outer edge of the bend, but then some way downtide, turn, and double back swimming into the current towards the inside of the bend and work that inner edge where the food gets pushed by the tide flow. Remember this – it's important if you want bass.

MUD FLATS, SIDE CHANNELS AND CREEKS

When an estuary is very shallow with mud flats, look to fish the slightly deeper channels that the water runs off through – these might only be a few inches deeper than the surrounding ground. These also bring the fish in initially as the tide floods and baits positioned here will catch fish. Once the tide is nearing full height the fish are widespread on the mud flats and are less easy to specifically target.

Often overlooked, side channels and creeks can give excellent returns.

STARTING POINT...

Always start at the mouth of a side channel or creek as the tide starts to push through. Keep low and don't make a profile of your body against the lighter horizon. The bass, mullet and flounders are literally right at the tide's edge as it floods into the channel or creek. Drop a crab bait here and you will soon have a fish on.

Again, look to the sides of the channels and creek to find the fish. Weedy areas, broken shingle and boulders, high mud banks, old and existing mooring tyres and chains will all see fish come nosing looking for a feed. The bends of the creek will fish well, especially on the inside where the current is slacker.

Where two creeks or channels meet and divide is another hotspot. The tide run will be much less this far off the main estuary, and flounders tend to sit at these junctions – either in the deepest part of the channel, or on the steeper inclines of the creek's flanks. In summer you can often disturb big flounders sunning themselves on these banks in the mid-afternoon. The fish return to these roosts to feed as the tide floods in, and especially at night.

Mullet also work the edges of the creeks, scooping mud up to take small food particles out. They will also frequent deeper pools and areas where sluice gates drain fields of freshwater.

Man-Made Structures

In many estuaries the first man-made structure you come to is a breakwater leading into a small harbour. Fish the breakwater right down the side into the boulders for bass, wrasse, congers and mini species. Again, these will be right under the rod tip and not more than a few yards out. If the base of the breakwater gives in to very shallow water, the best fishing can be just as the new flood tide pushes along the base of the rocks for bass and flounders. If the depth is much greater and never uncovers the base, then the flood tide and high water will be best for the wrasse and congers.

At end of the breakwater you will see that the tide flows around it strongly. This current will always hold bass downtide of the end of the breakwater. Trot a frozen sandeel under a float through here, or spin an artificial eel or lure, and you should do well.

If the harbour is shallow, check out the buoys identifying the deeper channel into the harbour, which guides the boats in, or

Cast bait near bridge supports because the fish will be hunting here.

Man-made structure is a great fish attractor because food such as prawns, crabs and shellfish will live around it.

Where two creeks or channels meet and divide is an excellent fish-holding spot.

Top tips

Take notice of which boats land fish and clean their decks down by the harbour wall. This area will hold flatfish, bass and mullet when the boat activity dies down in the evenings.

just watch the boat activity. The flanks of this deeper channel are good places to put baits for plaice, flounders, bass and even the odd ray if the water is deep enough.

Bridges across estuaries always concentrate the tide flow so, again, look for areas of fast flowing tide and expect to catch bass on float and spinning gear.

As a new flood tide reaches the bridge supports, drop crab baits in and around these to locate the bass that always investigate these structures, which are home to varied food such as crabs, mussel and small fish. The bigger flatfish tend to be on the flanks of the estuary just downtide of the bridge supports where the tide flow is weaker.

CONCLUSION

Reading the ground and the flow of the tide can tell you much about where the fish will be. In a nutshell you're looking for anything that breaks up the monotony of a straight running channel and pinpointing visually where food will collect as it gets pushed along by the tide.

The beauty about estuaries is that the fish, such as bass, are predictable and you can learn to get a fish or two from one mark, then move up the estuary a few hundred yards and ambush them again maximising your chances of sport.

Bass also come into the estuary with the tide, but then run out again to begin the cycle all over. This in and out migration gives you two chances to catch them. Bass feed just as heavily on the ebb tide as they do on the flood.

After reading and absorbing this feature, with time and experience you gain a trained eye that can spot fish-holding features at a glance.

The Heavy-Duty Conger Sliding-Leger Boat Rig

TSF reveals some of the best sea angling traces for you to use.

The origin of this rig has been lost in the past. Its basic form has certainly been around since the mid-1800s and probably way before that. It's one of the most common rigs used by experienced boat anglers because it targets a wide variety of species, and has been adopted as the classic big-conger rig when fishing into reef grounds and wrecks.

This wreck-conger rig has changed over the years, though – modern components have dramatically improved its efficiency. It also now includes a key mid-section between the hook and the main line or leader, which will become clear in the 'How It Works' section.

How It Works

It's crucial to understand the importance of the short section of 120lb mono that the sliding boom slides onto. It serves several purposes. Firstly it extends the hook trace where it meets wreckage and rough ground on the sea bed, it protects the main line or leader from any abrasion caused during a long fight with a big conger, and it gives you the advantage over a spooky conger that's only playing with the bait, as giving just a foot or so of line can often encourage the eel to fully take.

Many anglers make the mistake of using a swivel as the running link instead of a slider boom. Being a metal eye with a thin diameter this not only creates undue stress on the mono leader, but also the thin-wire eye diameter doesn't slide on the mono as efficiently as the boom does. This is because the boom spreads the load over a much wider area, increasing the ability of the rig to give line smoothly, reducing the chance of

an eel spooking.

The combined length of the 120lb and 200lb mono at roughly six-and-a-half feet also means that when a big conger is on the surface, the crewman can hold the eel on the heavy mono with the fish still safely on the surface of the water until the man with the gaff or net can secure it.

Another common mistake is to use a hook trace that's too long. This can allow the eel to take the bait and move back inside the wreck without the angler being aware of it.

Even for big congers a finished hook trace about 30 inches long is ideal. It gives the eel room to take the bait, but it can't back away very far before you feel the increase in tension. This early warning system can be vital when targeting big wreck congers – it gets them out of their holes before they realise what's happening.

It's also important to make sure that the mono you use has a hard surface

Build Sequence

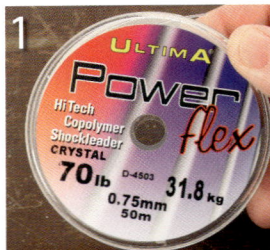

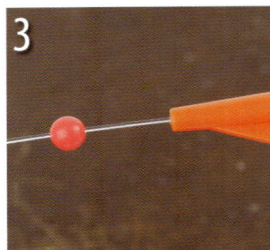

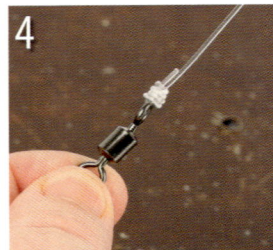

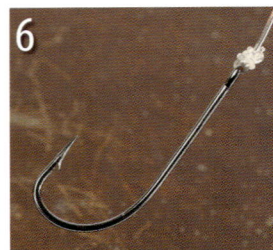

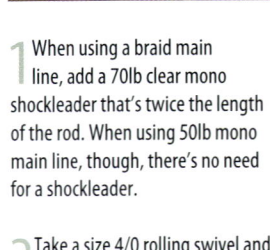

1. When using a braid main line, add a 70lb clear mono shockleader that's twice the length of the rod. When using 50lb mono main line, though, there's no need for a shockleader.

2. Take a size 4/0 rolling swivel and tie on a 48in length of 120lb clear mono using a four-turn uni knot.

3. Slide on a short zip slider to the lead, followed by an 8mm bead.

4. Tie the free end of the 120lb mono to another size 4/0 rolling swivel.

5. The hook trace is 30 inches of 200lb clear mono. Tie this to the size 4/0 swivel using a four-turn uni knot.

6. The hook is a size 8/0 to 10/0 Mustad 3406 O'Shaughnessy or a Partridge Sea Beast. Again use a four-turn uni knot to secure the hook to the mono.

7. To the link on the zip slider, add a short length of telephone wire or a short section of light mono as a weak link should the lead weight get snagged

but remains semi-supple. Some heavier line strengths are quite soft nowadays and they tend to allow the eel to bite through them more easily than a hard, slightly stiffer commercial-grade mono. To check this, press a fingernail onto the surface of the mono and see how easily it marks – simple, but a good tip!

Some anglers prefer to crimp the heavy mono to the swivels and hook eye, but this is unnecessary because the four-turn uni knot or a Domhoff is very secure when tied correctly in heavy mono.

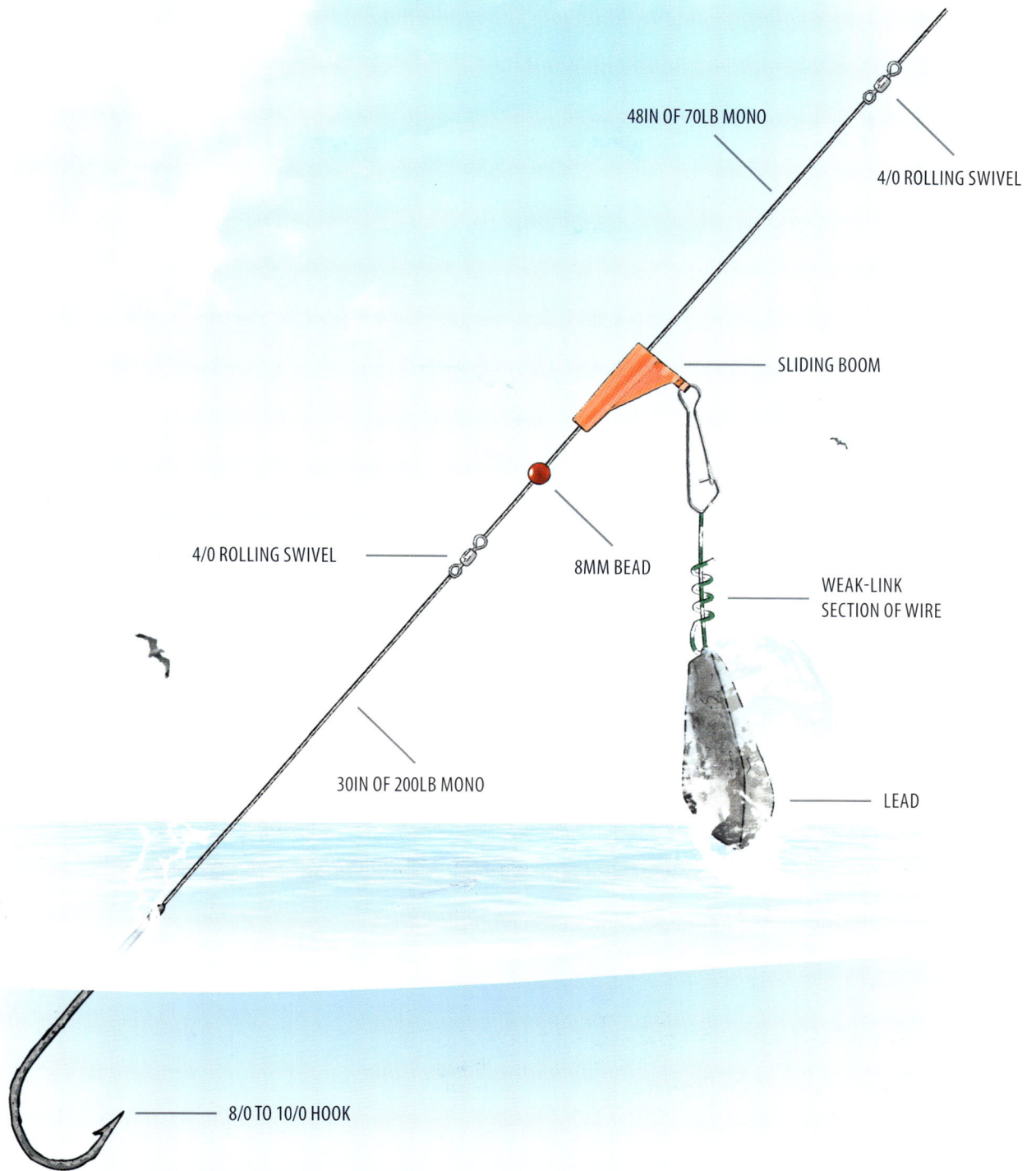

48IN OF 70LB MONO

4/0 ROLLING SWIVEL

SLIDING BOOM

4/0 ROLLING SWIVEL

8MM BEAD

WEAK-LINK
SECTION OF WIRE

30IN OF 200LB MONO

LEAD

8/0 TO 10/0 HOOK

Great fishing starts and finishes on-line.

Beach Rods • Beach Reels • Boat Rods • Boat Reels • Lure Rods • Lure Reels • Clothing • Boots • Waterproofs • Flotation • Shelters